T0072381

BORN
TO
Create

NEUROHACKING TO BREAK FREE!

DR. TIFFANY TAJIRI

WESTBOW
PRESS®
A DIVISION OF THOMAS NELSON
& ZONDERVAN

WestBow Press books may be ordered through booksellers or by contacting:

WestBow Press
A Division of Thomas Nelson & Zondervan
1663 Liberty Drive
Bloomington, IN 47403
www.westbowpress.com
844-714-3454

Scripture quotations are taken from the New King James Version. Copyright © 1982 by Thomas Nelson, Inc. Used by permission. All rights reserved.

ISBN: 979-8-3850-1005-9 (sc)
ISBN: 979-8-3850-1004-2 (e)

Library of Congress Control Number: 2023919502

Print information available on the last page.

WestBow Press rev. date: 12/06/2023

DEDICATION

To my compassionate, brilliant, and goofy son, Kai—may you read this book and learn how wonderfully God designed you. May it fill you with excitement about the amazing things that you will create. Enjoy the adventure of discovering your divine design for your divine destiny. Remember, it is the love of God that will guide you, abundantly provide for you, and bring your heart's highest calling to completion. I love you.

To my fairytale prince on a white horse, Alex—you are my rock and my comfort. Thank you for believing in my wildest dreams. You are a dream come true—an answered prayer. This book would not exist without you. Your presence in my life has radically shifted my world. I cherish you and love you beyond measure.

To my Wonder Woman, Mommy—thank you for teaching me to dream big. You continue to demonstrate that anything is possible when you operate in the love of God. You are an incredible role model and my greatest cheerleader since the day I took my first breath. I love you.

To my charismatic, Dad—thank you for being so incredibly present in this chapter of my life. You truly get me. We are connected deeply and profoundly in spirit. I love you.

To my Omi and Opa—thank you for creating the warmest and most joyful childhood memories. Your love and devotion gave me wings to soar to heights I could have never imagined—and the best is yet to come. I love you both for all of eternity.

CONTENTS

THE HERO'S JOURNEY BEGINS...

PART I: THE CALL TO ADVENTURE

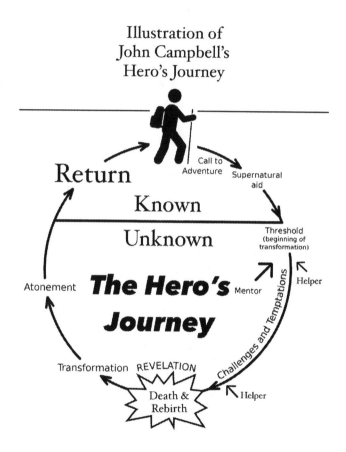

Illustration of
John Campbell's
Hero's Journey

INTRODUCTION

"That's the real trouble with the world, too many people grow up."

WALT DISNEY

LIKE A GIDDY CHILD, I simply cannot keep a secret when it involves gifting someone I love. It's absolute torture. Hence, my surprises for others only come to fruition when a spontaneous idea enters my brain less than 48 hours prior to the celebrated occasion, such as a birthday or anniversary. Then I race against the clock to make it all happen. The moment my surprise comes to life, I revel in the joy and excitement that overcomes my loved one, savoring the magical connection like I savor the last slice of birthday cake—so delicious!

Speaking of birthdays, it was my son's seventh birthday when we pulled Kai out of school for a "medical appointment." He crawled into his car seat dreading what he imagined would end in a vaccination and a "lame" safety pop. At that moment, I was struck by pixie dust, and I transformed into seven-year-old Tiffany. "Just kidding!" I shouted as my husband, Alex, captured the event on video. "We're going to the happiest place on Earth!" My son looked at me with disdain and with an exasperated sigh replied, "The doctor is not the happiest place on Earth, Mom!" Alex and I smiled wide at one another, not surprised by our son's sarcasm. We lingered on the precipice of surprise—it was like waiting for the beat to drop when listening to your favorite song. "No, silly!" Alex replied. "We are going to

Disneyland!" He articulated each syllable of the word. The energy of that statement landed with so much force that it quite literally blew my son's mind, rendering him jaw-dropping speechless. As you can imagine, this surprise was dreamt up 48 hours prior to that magical moment.

As the wheels of the plane lifted, so did my spirit. I intentionally broke free from the ball and chain that was a toxic work environment and a state of chronic stress. I was putting distance and time between the old version of me and this new version that I was now about to embrace as I put on my flashy Mickey Mouse ears and entered the gates to Disneyland. Here, everyone has permission to be their seven-year-old self; here, dreams come true; here, is the happiest place on earth; here, I am limitless; here, I am reunited with old friends, the Disney characters, who fill me with hope; here, I am in a time capsule of nostalgia; here, is where I break free! It's my choice.

My biology changed that weekend because I chose to break the cycle to create a new experience. My renewed mindset and emotional elation pushed dopamine and oxytocin throughout my body. This was a beautiful respite from all the stress hormones that surged throughout my body on a regular basis. Changing my beliefs quite literally changed my biology and in doing so, I set free my creative, inner child from the dismal dungeon of chronic stress and boy, did it feel good. That weekend, my aura was so bright it could be seen from outer space, seriously!

Lost in awe, I watched Kai and Alex wearing their Goofy and Mickey hats, holding hands, excitedly rushing from one ride to the next. There was so much to do and so little time—stress was replaced with exhilaration. For both, this was their very first experience at a Disney park, and they allowed themselves to be fully swept away by the magic. Alex is a retired Soldier who served nearly 30 years in the Army and partook in four combat tours to Iraq and Afghanistan. I tell you this because if a tough warrior like him can choose to surrender to the spirit of the child, anyone can. It's a choice that we have every day—that we deny on most occasions. Why do we starve, lock away, and isolate our inner child? What happened to the magic? Where did all the creative energy go?

And with the blink of an eye, the wheels touched the ground on the runway of our hometown. My inner child begrudgingly moped her way back into her dungeon, dragging my bright and shiny aura with her. She locked herself in and handed me the key—no telling when she would be set free again. A lump formed in my throat and all I could think about was the pile of problems that accumulated in my absence from work—the sort of surprises that I despise. My brain is a dutiful chemist, creating the neurochemical experience that I instruct it to create. The stress hormones coursed through my veins like an old and toxic addiction that took my breath away in all the wrong ways. Just like Cinderella, I got caught up in the all-too-short magical frenzy and I left something behind—something very important. "Back to life. Back to reality..." was the 90s ballad by Soul II Soul that reverberated in my head on repeat.

I share this story because even as a Doctor of Clinical Psychology, a community leader, a published author, and an Air Force Veteran, I was stuck in the vortex that leads too many of us down a spiral headed toward disease and eventually death. I lost my passion and my purpose. It was like a vampire had sucked me dry. It wasn't until my mid-30s that I recognized I needed to radically change the way I live my life and how I experience it if I'm ever going to feel whole again. Feeling whole is just the starting point to feeling limitless and eventually living out your wildest dreams.

In this book you will learn about the incredible power of your mind and how to harness it to create the life of your dreams. We will journey all the way back to your childhood to evaluate the programs that you downloaded from the world and determine if they are in line with the vibration of your future self. If not, we will work on downloading new programs. This is a spiritual journey. In this process, you will come to see that you were created and designed to live a life bursting with love and abundance. But to get there, you will have to become aware of how you got to where you are. There is no turning back once you become aware—because you can never become unaware again.

Those who have zero desire to level up will tell you that "ignorance is bliss." Let me be the first to call it as I see it—"chosen ignorance" is "stuck on senseless." You cannot create to your fullest potential when you are stuck. Learning the basics of neuroscience, epigenetics, and quantum physics will help you understand how you were designed and will further reinforce the fact that you have the power within you to be an incredible creator, sharing your unique gifts with the world. It is your divine right after all.

Allow me to share another story about my son. The dental hygienist asked him if he wanted a balloon. In a cool, calm, and collected manner, he said, "No, thank you." I raised my hand and asked if I could have his balloon instead. Kai turned red from both frustration and embarrassment, and he replied, "Moooooooommm!!!" The dental hygienist smiled and said, "Of course! What color?" I got my purple balloon, but with it came sadness because my son was truly self-conscious. When we got back to the car, I explained to him that I am spending the rest of my life teaching adults how to embrace their inner child and to find freedom in fun, play, creativity, imagination, and adventure because this is our inherent nature. This childlike outlook is what brightens our electromagnetic signature, our aura, that communicates directly with the universe. It is a limitless state of mind with a frequency and vibration that activates, for our benefit, the laws of the universe. After my discourse, quite literally those exact words, my son looked at me wide-eyed, nodded, and stole the balloon from me!

Let's revisit the concept of Disney for a moment. So many of us, no matter our demographics, are attracted to the world of Disney because it speaks to our inner child, while its stories resound with a truth that we are mysteriously drawn to. Remember hearing this? "We shall know the truth, and the truth shall set us free..." Disney stories resonate so profoundly at a subconscious level because every plot at its core reflects the law of attraction, the law of vibration, the spirit of harmony, the law of faith, and above all true love. I'm not saying Disney is perfect— it doesn't have to be, just like we don't have to be perfect. Superficial human perfection is an illusion created to cause chaos and dysfunction, separating us from our highest self and from one another. Only true love is perfect, and it resides deeply and profoundly within us—and within our favorite Disney movies.

The skeptics will sum it up by saying, "Disney is predictable—the good guys always win!" That statement is true of Disney and of real life, whether we see it in this dimension or the next. Love is a self-organizing intelligence that works hand-in-hand with the spirit of harmony to create beauty from ashes. All chaos will eventually become organized. Most of us can agree that explosions create the ultimate kind of destruction—physical chaos. Let's rewind back to the Big Bang—the mother of all explosions—and look at where we are at now! We are considerably organized with majestic skylines, soaring skyscrapers, and incredible natural wonders. All things will eventually work for the good of those who fall in line with love and truth. To quote Descartes, "We are spiritual beings having a human experience." Let's break it down—think of spiritual as multi-dimensional and human as linear. If we approach it from another perspective, we could say that we were not designed to be linear beings living linear lives; we were designed to be dimensional beings living dimensional lives. Doesn't that sound amazing? This is how our power to create sets us apart from any other species on the planet.

You are the hero in your story or will be by the end of this book. Together, we will journey with our favorite Disney characters and examine their lives, their obstacles, their surrender, and their victory, as we reinforce their experiences through the lens of science and spirit. Whether we like it or not, these characters have been our babysitters and our children's babysitters. Whether during our childhood or adulthood, we have endured their trials and triumphs alongside them. They are characters that we have become attached to even though they are only a part of our imagination—which only goes to show how powerful our imagination is. It is safe to use their stories as case studies as we dissect our lives alongside theirs.

I am pleased to say that I have found what I left behind at Disneyland. In fact, I wouldn't be writing this book if I hadn't found it. You also have everything you need to create the life of your dreams. It's time to dust it off, rewire it, deprogram it, reprogram it, and neurohack it to become limitless. Buckle up because you are about to embark on the Hero's journey. After all, you were born to create!

"It's kind of fun to do the impossible."

WALT DISNEY

Chapter 1

THE BIG PICTURE

"First, think. Second, dream. Third, believe. And finally, dare."

WALT DISNEY

Tootsie Roll Pop

IS THERE A RIGHT WAY to eat a Tootsie Roll Pop? Absolutely! The wrong way to eat a Tootsie Roll Pop is to impatiently chomp down on the chocolatey center, and then savagely gnaw at the candy that crumbles around your mouth and falls onto the floor. The proper way to eat it is to patiently lick off the hard candy shell and then savor the chewy, gooey, chocolatey center. This ensures that every morsel of candy gets eaten and not wasted. I write this to make the point that this book is organized in such a fashion—from big picture to the details that comprise it. I find that when we understand how the big concepts work, we are better capable of comprehending the connections that allow them to function in the way that they do—without losing any important information. We would not want to attempt to put a puzzle together without ever having seen the picture that it creates. Now that I've made my point—feel free to chomp down on your Tootsie Roll Pop. I was only kidding—there is no wrong way to eat it! So, how many licks does it take to get to the center of a Tootsie Roll Pop? An average of 364 licks according to Purdue University!

The magical formula

Love is magical in all its forms. One may consider it the ultimate pixie dust that grants us the power to fly—and even soar! The chemicals of love on the mind, body, and spirit allow us to feel limitless as we operate in a realm of infinite possibilities. We become the author of an incredible story wherein we are the hero. This is our natural state, as we are neurobiologically wired to love and to be loved. It is the ultimate source of energy. When we flow in the vibration and frequency of love, anything is possible. The Walt Disney Company knows this, capitalizes on it, and cashes in. We will spend any amount of money on things that we believe will create love, inspire love, attract love, enhance love, or allow us to vicariously experience love. Love is the greatest driving force in all the universe. Don't worry, I will back these statements with neuroscientific facts in the pages to come.

Illustration of
John Campbell's
Hero's Journey

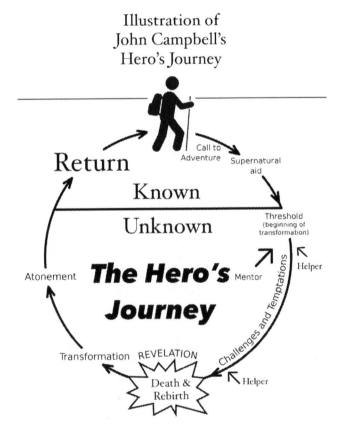

You are about to embark on the Hero's journey. This is a monomyth or a template that Disney producers use to develop the storylines of their movies. In fact, it is also the algorithm to becoming our ideal self, as it demands that we have the courage to let go of the known in exchange for the unknown, in hopes of fantastic possibilities. The journey ends when we've become awakened to a new way of life wherein truth and love preside—and where truth and love preside, peace always follows. At a subconscious level, your spirit has known this algorithm all along, and that is why Disney movies resonate so profoundly with so many of us.

Unfortunately, most of us only embark on the Hero's journey when we have reached our limit of misfortunes. Ironically, living in chaos and discord can become our comfort zone, and most people opt for this chaotic state over undergoing the discomfort of transformation for the possibility of a better tomorrow. The pursuit of the unknown conjures up the emotion of fear—love's antithesis. "There is no fear in love. But perfect love drives out fear…" Fear is the second greatest driving force in all the universe.

Moana, Wreck-it Ralph, Remy, Elsa and Anna, Ariel, the Incredibles, and all the Disney heroes that you can name decided that the risk of the unknown was worth taking, considering their dire circumstances. If they chose to remain stuck, they would live inauthentically, and it would drain them of their essence, as they would miss their hearts' highest calling and perfect self-expression. One may say that these characters have hit rock bottom—like Ralph in *Wreck-it Ralph*. He felt stuck, miserable, and depressed playing the role of the "bad guy" in his video game. JK Rowling stated, "Rock bottom became the solid foundation on which I rebuilt my life." Rebuilding is choosing to no longer live in the rubble of destruction, instead choosing to step into the unknown, where infinite and incredible possibilities abound.

Once our Disney characters muster the courage to journey into the unknown, they are pleasantly surprised to receive love's supernatural guidance. But to be guided, they must surrender to love. This surrender requires faith and trust that love will always make a way to our heart's highest calling, even when the "going gets tough"—and it gets tough, I assure you. "Nothing worth having comes easy," said Theodore Roosevelt. Once these characters surrender, they begin to flow with the laws of the universe (laws of faith, harmony, attraction, non-resistance, karma, grace, and vibration), all of which are governed by the self-organizing intelligence that is love. For those inclined to religion—consider that the Creator of the universe is the One who created the laws, as they are also found in scripture.

We must lose our expectations to receive love's supernatural guidance because it comes in many forms, and we may miss it if we are too rigid in our thinking. Grimsby in the 2023 version of *The Little Mermaid* instructs Prince Eric in the same manner: "Don't be held back by what you think should be. Think of only what is."

Love's supernatural guidance came in the form of an animated ocean for Moana, a magical snowman for Anna, a wacky and wise seamstress for the Incredibles, and a ghost chef for Remy. Auguste Gusteau (ghost chef) appears to Remy while he is stealing food from a kitchen in Paris and says, "A cook makes, and a thief takes. Food will come. Food will always come to those who love to cook." Auguste Gusteau's supernatural guidance reminds Remy of the law of faith and the law of attraction—while he is in his darkest hour. Did the food eventually come? Of course—he had more food than he could have ever imagined, guessed, or requested in his wildest dreams. In her first encounter with Prince Eric, Ariel's spirit instantaneously knew that she would someday live the life of her dreams if she had the courage to pursue the uncharted territories of becoming human. She literally sings, "I don't know when, and I don't know how, but I know that something is starting right now. Watch and you'll see, someday I'll be part of that world." Loud and clear, she declares her trust in the supernatural to manifest exactly what she desires, while radiating a bright and shiny aura that communicates her desire like a magnet to the universe.

The death of the old self and the view of the world as we once knew it is inevitable. This remarkable transformation results in a rebirth of a new and authentic self-image that is accompanied by a refreshing world view anchored in truth and inspired by love. Atonement follows this transformation. This is where the new version of you reconciles with all the elements (people, places, situations) of your past to instill peace and harmony for a new beginning. Holding on to negative emotional energy tends to obstruct your blessings because you remain guarded when you should be open to receive. This means that you must confront the source of your hurt and free yourself from that pain. You must break free from any negative energetic attachments to step fully into your divine calling.

This is where Remy becomes the chef of his dreams, and his talent blows the minds of his critics—perhaps, I should've said "blows their tastebuds!" This is where Ariel marries Prince Eric and her mermaid family unites with the humans, creating a peaceful alliance between land and ocean. This is where Wreck-it Ralph discovers love in a newfound friendship outside of his game, and recognizes that being a hero comes from within, not from being awarded a shiny medal. Do you see how the formula plays out?

The new challenge is to remain in this "awakened state" and take everything that you've learned into your future. You will continue to manifest great things—the goodness will keep coming—if you believe. The Hero's journey continues to repeat itself throughout our lifetime as we learn and grow. But it gets easier each time because you have discovered the rhythm of the universe, and you have proof of the power of love to do incredible things—that's how faith is born! This constant evolution makes for fantastic Disney sequels. You were born to create and to make all your dreams come true—because the world is in desperate need of what only you can offer. You possess a divine design for your divine destiny. If you don't believe me, believe Disney: "No matter how your heart is grieving, if you keep on believing, the dream that you wish will come true."

Shine brightly

How brightly do you shine? Everything in our material universe is constantly emitting light and information in the form of energy. This light is called an electromagnetic signature, also known as an aura. An electromagnetic signature is the result of energy vibrating at a particular frequency. Everything is comprised of atoms and atoms vibrate at different speeds in different forms, from solids, to liquids, to gases.

Joy is my second favorite all-time Disney character from the movie *Inside Out,* which is about our emotions. Each emotion is depicted as a fun-loving character—Joy, Disgust, Anger, Fear, and Sadness. If you pay close attention to Joy, you will notice that she is the character with the brightest electromagnetic signature, as she appears to glow throughout the movie. There is so much truth to this depiction because positive emotions such as joy, happiness, and love shine brighter than negative emotions. Some researchers say that our aura can project approximately ten feet from the location of our heart.

A combination of our thoughts and emotions creates our electromagnetic signature—these are the vibrations of our body. How does it work? These vibrations vibrate at a specific frequency and each frequency has an associated sound and color. Such vibrations cannot be seen by the untrained eye. In fact, you may have felt the energy of a person passing you on the street or even felt the shift in energy when an important person walks into a room. Some energies are magnetic and attractive, while others can be repulsive.

Negative emotions, such as fear and anger, draw energy from our electromagnetic signature, dimming its vibrance. Chronic stress sucks the life out of us. In fact, the electromagnetic signature of an inanimate object shines as brightly as does that of someone in a state of chronic stress. Our electromagnetic signature is powerful and influences every cell in our body, as well as our material world. The color and intensity of our electromagnetic signature reflects our health and the flow of energy within our bodies. What color are you? How brightly do you shine?

Universal rhythm and the law of attraction

Everything produces after its own kind: Your electromagnetic signature is the information you project to the universe. It is both electric and magnetic, as it draws to you everything congruent with the state of your thinking and feeling. Another way to think of its function is like a boomerang. The stronger your emotional vibration, the more powerful the energy you broadcast, which means the more influence you have over the material world. Your electromagnetic signature is the gateway to manifestation through the law of attraction. Here are some famous words about this phenomenon...

"The universe is worked and guided from within outwards."
Helena Blavatsky

"For as a person thinks, so are they." Proverbs 23:7

"Belief in limitation is the one and only thing that causes limitation." Thomas Troward

One golden nugget that you absolutely need to know is that *everything produces after its own kind.* This can be as concrete as a dog produces (gives birth) a dog, or a watermelon seed produces a watermelon. But it can also be as abstract as energy, emotions, thoughts, and intentions. When you push positive energy out into the world through acts of love, it comes right back to you in different forms—from smiles to random acts of kindness. Positive thoughts grounded in belief and action boomerang into open doors filled with opportunity. The reverse of that is true too.

Self-fulfilling prophecy: Negative self-thoughts often lead to unintentional self-sabotage. *Self-fulfilling prophecy* is when this universal rhythm pertains to our own thoughts and beliefs about ourselves. It is a psychological phenomenon that occurs when we "believe" something about ourselves, positive or negative, and our behaviors produce the outcome of our belief. Moreover, our electromagnetic signature draws to us the people, situations, or things of the material world that are equivalent to our thinking and feeling. Negative thoughts of our subconscious mind often become our 3D experience. One who self-sabotages may reply, "See! I told you I couldn't do it!" Well, you couldn't do it, because you believed that you couldn't do it—and you attracted an experience congruent with what you believed! How about that? Believe. Behave. Become!

Have you ever had one of those days when you woke up angry at the world? Your clothes don't fit right. You don't like how you look or feel. You're running late. You snap at the people you live with. Your negative energy (thoughts, emotions, and behavior) brings about more chaos. For example, while in your car, you may back into your garage door in a rush, then you get pulled over for running a stop sign, then your coffee spills all over your clothes as you try to make the meeting on time—it's a domino effect of negativity. Many people call it "a case of the Mondays!"

Why? Because most people feel reluctant to start another week of school or work. Many begin dreading Monday during the latter half of Sunday. This depressed and anxious outlook feels chaotic and attracts chaos.

Neural programming: There are scientists who propose that the law of attraction takes place in the subconscious mind with neuroanatomy tied to the reticular activating system. This area of the brain has many responsibilities, but it is best known for controlling our sleep and wake cycles, as well as some aspects of survival. It is the subconscious mind that runs the programs that we downloaded into our brain between the ages of 0-7 years. These programs are like algorithms for how we view ourselves, others, and the world at large, dictating how we think, feel, and behave. Many of us have dysfunctional programs that we are operating on every single day, and we are unaware of how they are negatively impacting our life. Remember the self-fulfilling prophecy? What if I told you that most of us are operating in our subconscious mind for over 95% of our lives? It's true. What do you think I will attract if I believe that I am unworthy? What do you think my electromagnetic signature will look like? We will explore this further in the pages to come.

Does all this apply to animals? Dr. Rene Peoc'h investigated whether the law of attraction was applicable to animals as it is to humans. When chicks hatch, they imprint on their mother and follow her like a shadow. However, if the mother is not present during the time they hatch, the chicks will imprint on the first moving object that crosses their path. Dr. Rene Peoc'h built a robot that was programmed with a random event generator that determined where it would travel in an arena. It was designed to go left and right 50% of the time, equally covering the length of both sides of the arena. You guessed it: Dr. Rene Peoc'h exposed the newly hatched chicks to the robot and allowed them to imprint on it. As you can imagine, the robot had the chicks equally covering the length of the arena and as they followed the robot they chirped "mama, mama." Okay, just checking to make sure you're still following me—no pun intended. After the chicks imprinted on the robot, he placed them in a transparent container at one end of the arena. The chicks were able to watch the robot from their location. What happened next was astounding—the desire of the chicks to be near the robot was so powerful that it had a significant influence on the random event generator. It no longer covered equal ground in the arena but remained in the half of the arena closest to the chicks. If the strong desire of the chicks can influence the movements of a machine, just imagine the incredible power you possess to attract the future of your dreams.

The power of believing: The law of attraction is deactivated in the presence of doubt and disbelief, which are both feelings and beliefs derived from the emotion of fear. In 1954 physicians and physiologists made it known that they believed it to be physically impossible to run a mile in under four minutes—no had done it. On a rainy and overcast day, Roger Bannister decided to give it a try. The track he ran on was slick and less than ideal. Moreover, he was enrolled in medical school at the time! For anyone who has been through graduate school, you can probably agree that physical fitness takes the back burner to studying. Nevertheless, Roger ran the mile in under four minutes because he believed he could do it! That is fantastic in and of itself, but the true "awe and wonder" came immediately after the world record was broken. Only a few days later, several runners ran the mile in under four minutes—why? Because this time, they believed it was possible—and so it was. Oh, there's that self-fulfilling prophecy again—this time in a positive direction!

If you want supernatural results, play by the rules of the supernatural: Thoughts are the language of your brain, while emotions are the language of your body, and together they create your electromagnetic signature—the light that broadcasts to the universe. Your message to the material world is a comprehensive experience of the mind, body, and spirit. Manifestation is the process of using the law of attraction to obtain your desires. It is truly an art form that is grounded in love and requires us to elevate our thinking and our feeling, all while possessing faith without limits. It is NOT wishing for a million dollars to land on your doorstep within 24 hours. There are rules to be followed. The universe will support your manifestation when you allow love to guide your decisions and your actions. You will attract immeasurable abundance in your life when you can...

- Love others
- Live in truth and honesty
- Listen to and learn from others

- Seek peace
- Take responsibility
- Possess an open mind
- Demonstrate compassion
- Lay down your ego
- Allow new experiences into your life
- Live by a moral compass
- Give generously without expectation
- Embrace flexible thinking
- Be patient
- Demonstrate dedication and motivation
- Value and love yourself
- Release negative emotional energy
- Listen to your intuition
- Embrace an abundant mindset
- Set healthy boundaries

When these conditions are met, and you identify a dedicated decision about what your heart desires (thought) and you elevate your emotion to match that desire, watch your dreams unfold before your eyes. Manifestation is far more than a wish—it demands action on your part! In fact, it demands that you become the receiver of what you desire to receive before you receive it. That sounds tricky; reread that sentence again. Most people practice the *fantastic feeling* of gratitude for this reason. You emote gratitude for what you believe is yours before it is yours. You attract what you are! If you are the vibrational match to what you desire, congratulations, it's yours. It is impossible to attract what you are not—it's the law!

Get ready! Here's another tip or trick to get what is divinely yours. Get ready! Get ready! Get ready! Make the necessary preparations to receive what you desire. You must make room for what you ask for, even when there is no sign of it. When you do this, you demonstrate your faith. Florence Scovel Shinn wrote in her book, *The Game of Life & How to Play It,* "If you ask for success and prepare for failure you will get what you have prepared for." She described a situation wherein a woman had no money for Christmas gifts for her family and feared that the tree would be empty. Florence instructed the woman to give thanks for the many presents under her Christmas tree prior to receiving them. As an act of faith, she also encouraged this woman to purchase the wrapping paper and bows needed to decorate the presents. Just before Christmas, the woman received a large sum of money that was owed to her, and her tree was littered with multiple gifts for everyone. Get ready, my friend. It's coming…

Love

For the purpose of this book, let us define love as the most powerful universal energy, which provides comfort, fulfillment, order, and peace. You are neurobiologically wired to love and to be loved. Love is most often observed as a transfer of energy between intelligent beings. What many fail to see is that love is a spiritual energy that resides within all of us. Like an aquifer, if you turn inward and dig deep enough, you can tap into it to fill every void in your life. Love is divine and it is the true essence of our being, as it is the source. Just as our electronic device must be plugged into an outlet to charge so that it may function in the way that it was designed, you must also plug into the source of love to be charged and to function in the way that you were designed. Once plugged in, the source becomes your guide, as it fulfills you and provides for you in all ways. The laws of the universe will only work in your favor when you are plugged into the source. Love is supernatural and so are you.

Some may define perfect love in a spiritual capacity between themselves and their creator. Biblical scripture states that "God is love. Whoever lives in love lives in God and God in them." Human love at its best is spiritual—magical! Even when people who love one another make mistakes, they aim to understand each other with compassion and work to improve "how" they show their love through their interactions. The best version of ourselves strives to push the love forward, and in doing so, we embrace our spiritual self.

Whatever you do, never mistake love as weak—it is the most powerful force. In fact, love has a strong backbone, and it sets healthy boundaries with forces that aim to wreak havoc upon it. Love is not unconditional tolerance for the abusive behaviors of others. When our spiritual self loves and accepts the human self and vice versa, respect is formed. Self-respect guides us away from toxic energy and chaos. Love is not defined by your dysfunctional relationships. You will come to learn that love is truly selfless, free, without obligation, safe, comforting, always present—never abandoning, fulfilling, satisfying, pure, just, kind, lovely, and patient.

In today's world, many of us have a twisted perception of love based on the way we were treated as children by those who were "supposed" to love us. In time, we will heal from those experiences and come to recognize love as it is defined by this book. Suffice it to say all of us have experienced the energetic force of love even if our home life was a disaster. Love may come in the form of a compliment from a stranger, from our teacher when we were in grade school, from a pet, from a friend, etc. Later in this book we will address the neuroscience behind attachment, so that you can identify what attachment style you gravitate toward and why, whether that attachment style is worthy of taking into your future, and how to deprogram and reprogram a new attachment style, if necessary.

Why do we suffer?

Because we are alive, psychological suffering is inevitable. No one is immune to the suffering of this world—not even the most revered spiritual persons in all of history (Jesus, Buddha, Mohammed, etc.). You will soon come to understand that you can only serve one master—love (which beholds faith) or fear. Human suffering falls into two categories: the category of *loss*, which includes death (if you don't believe in spiritual eternity) and destruction, followed by the category of *selfish* or cruel acts.

Remember, you are neurobiologically wired to love and to be loved. I believe that love is the purpose of our creation. Foremost, love is a choice so it requires you to possess free will. You cannot have love without free will. If our free will were displayed as a spectrum of choices, one end of the spectrum would be *love*, and at the opposite end would be *fear*, the source of all selfish and cruel behavior.

Most of the hurt in this world occurs when we use our free will to be selfish and unkind. I believe it is safe to say that love is selfless and is aligned with light and order (syntropy) on one end of the spectrum, while selfishness is a derivative of fear and aligned with darkness and chaos (entropy) at the other end. Who would've known that *Star Wars* holds the answers to the existential underpinnings of universe? *May the Force be with you.*

At times we have been at the receiving end of someone's wickedness; at other times, we have been the source of it. You may have heard the saying, "People who are hurting, hurt other people." In short, "hurt people, hurt people." Will you choose to stop the vicious cycle? In the famous words of Dr. Martin Luther King, "Darkness cannot drive out darkness; only light can do that. Hate cannot drive out hate; only love can do that."

Remember, through the narrative lens that we create, we can turn our problems into power and our trials and tribulations into testimonies. This book will show you how. Our stories inspire hope and healing for others, and when we have the courage to share, we ignite a profound spiritual connection. Nietzsche said, *The meaninglessness of suffering, not suffering itself, was the curse that lay over mankind.* Choose to find meaning in your suffering and use that meaning as fuel to become your highest spiritual self.

Spirituality

I would be amiss to leave out the incredible spiritual component that makes you—YOU. As Pierre Teilhard de Chardin put it, *"We are not human beings having a spiritual experience. We are spiritual beings having a human experience."* When you understand this—and operate in this understanding—your mind becomes limitless. In the chapters to follow you will learn that all living energy is connected in the quantum realm. Think of its portrayal like Eywa, the biological sentient guiding and connecting the force of all life in the Avatar movies.

Spirituality acknowledges that there is something greater than our self that goes beyond our sensory experience as human beings and connects us to a greater whole, which we are a part of—something divine in nature. A spiritual perspective encourages embarking upon a meaningful life that excels past the mundane existence driven by biological needs and survival instinct. It recognizes that we are part of a purposeful unfolding and connects us to the loving intelligence of the universe. In yoga, one ends their class by saying "namaste," which translates to "the divine within me bows to the same divine within you."

Spirituality is an exploration of introspection on topics concerning love, existentialism (purpose), knowledge, truth, suffering, and even death. It provides context to all life circumstances—good, bad, and ugly. Living life through a spiritual lens helps to transcend suffering. Our faith can help us to find peace and safety even during life's most brutal storms.

A spiritual journey seeks to heal the self and to promote the healing of others. It is a journey that encourages you to operate at your purest level of love—tethered by grace and selflessness.

Born to create

As a psychologist, I have asked hundreds of patients this question: "What is your purpose in life? Or what is the meaning of life?" Surprisingly, most patients reacted to me as if I had suddenly and spontaneously grown another head. The common response was, "I haven't thought about that—I'm just trying to get through today." As an existential junkie, I could not fathom not knowing the answer to this question.

Humans are complicated. It is almost impossible to have a one-size-fits-all "life purpose." Yet the Japanese culture comes close in providing an operational definition of such a complex idea. If you are wondering what your purpose is, I propose a perspective from traditional Japanese medicine called Ikigai. This means "reason for being." If one can attain Ikigai, their life will be fulfilled. There are four primary goals that one must achieve to experience Ikigai:

- Do what you love
- Do what you are good at

- Do what you can be paid for
- Do what the world needs

This is just a taste of the incredible life that you can create. There are two words that are the same length and possess identical letters that are arranged in different orders—yet they operate on opposite ends of the spectrum of life. Which one are you, the REACTOR or the CREATOR? The reactor waits for the world to change them, while the creator initiates the change that needs to be made to become what they so fervently desire. You were born to create!

Process Questions

- ➢ Are you ready to embark upon the Hero's journey?
- ➢ What is holding you back from embarking upon the Hero's journey?
- ➢ How can you overcome those obstacles?
- ➢ Why is it important to begin the Hero's journey?
- ➢ Do you self-sabotage? If so, how?
- ➢ Reflect on experiences in your life that you identify as spiritual. How did they make you feel?
- ➢ How do you define love? Do you like your definition?
- ➢ Ikigai

  - ○ What do you love?
  - ○ What are you good at?
  - ○ What does the world need that you can provide?
  - ○ How can you monetize it?

- ➢ What do you want to create?

Freedom Rhythm

- ➢ Please turn to page 180 to read about Freedom Rhythm and how to perform it. A total of four Transformation Zones are meant to be practiced together. Transformation Zones 1, 2, and 4 are found on page 186. Each chapter will have a unique Transformation Zone 3 to be practiced in the set of four Transformation Zones.
- ➢ **Transformation Zone 3:**

  - ○ **Visualization with bilateral stimulation:** *I want you to search for the most magical moments in your life. Now, I want you to fully immerse yourself back into those magical moments as if they were happening right now!*

o The mindset that informs your creative movement:

- Dedicated Decision: "I am magical."
- Fantastic Feeling: "Child-like excitement."

o Creative movement: Now, put your experience into movement with your silk.

o Positive Affirmation: "I am magical! Yes, I am!" x 3

PART II: REVELATION

Illustration of
John Campbell's
Hero's Journey

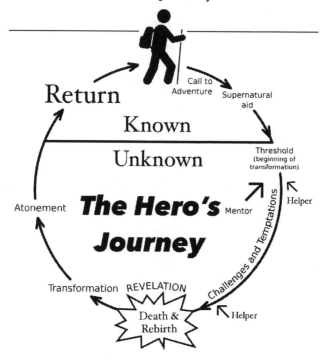

Chapter 2

LOVE VS. FEAR

"When you are curious, you find lots of interesting things to do."

WALT DISNEY

The power in you

MOST PEOPLE HAVE NO CLUE about how powerful their brain is. Let's reference this power in relatable terms. Since most of us have cellphones, think of it like this. Your brain generates more electrical impulses in one day than all the cellphones on the planet combined. Take a moment to absorb that statement and fathom how much energy that is. What is it about our brain that produces so much energy? Let me give you a hint: It's the same thing that creates your electromagnetic signature (aura)—your thoughts and emotions. Are you allowing the incredible energy of your brain to benefit you? Or is it being weaponized against you?

Your brain is simply a ball of globular goop—a big wad of spaghetti that rests inside your skull. This non-glamorous looking organ hosts approximately 80 billion brain cells known as neurons, and each neuron can make up to one thousand connections with other neurons. These connections are called neural networks. It is helpful for me to think of such neurons as stars and their connections as constellations. Just as constellations come together to form a visual story, neural networks come together to form thoughts, memories, emotions, and behaviors. The funny thing is that the number of neurons in our head is nearly equivalent to the number of stars in our galaxy. Each person's brain is like its own galaxy! But here is the real kicker: There is a difference between your mind vs. your brain even though they are a part of the same neuroanatomy.

Let's reference the Disney movie *Inside Out*. Riley is the main character and, in her head reside her primary emotions: Joy, Sadness, Anger, Disgust, and Fear which are depicted as fun-loving characters. Together, they operate in a high-tech environment wherein they have front row seats to observe everything that transpires in Riley's life—this location is called "Headquarters." Joy, Sadness, Anger, Disgust, and Fear take turns running a console that influences Riley's thoughts and behaviors. Riley's core memories create her five islands of personality— Family Island, Friendship Island, Goofball Island, Hockey Island, and Honesty Island—that float outside of headquarters but are connected via an intricate network of memory relay tunnels. Think of your mind as "Headquarters," while your brain is everything else, including all memories and the islands of personality.

Some say that your mind is your brain in action. It is responsible for being the brain's gatekeeper. It is your free will. What you choose to give your attention is what will shape your brain and become your experience from the *inside out*—no pun intended. Every moment of every day you are filtering what you allow into your brain and consequently what you put out. Your mind is both your conscious awareness and your attention. You may have heard the saying, "Where your attention goes, your energy flows."

Your mind always commands your brain—except when we are in survival mode, which we will address later. Moreover, your brain always commands your body without any exceptions. The mind tells the brain what to think, what to believe, and what to do in most circumstances— it even instructs the brain on what chemicals to produce and send throughout the body via the bloodstream. Then, like a puppet master, the brain carries out the instructions to the body via the central and peripheral nervous systems (the anatomical networks that connect the brain to the body).

This may sound like a wild concept to grasp—your brain does not know the difference between a real experience and an imagined (visualized) experience, yet your mind does. Your brain will lay down the same neural networks while imagining the experience as it does while physically doing the experience. Why do you think professional athletes always visualize their performance?

Moreover, your imagination is where all creation begins. It is a superpower granted solely to your mind. When your mind believes you are limitless, you become limitless. As soon as your mind believes you are limited, you become limited. When you joke about being ignorant or unlucky, your brain receives this information from the mind as a fact, and then it interprets this fact as an instruction to create the experience. Let me put it this way: Your brain has zero sense of humor. You may joke about being poor, deranged, or clueless—and your brain will literally interpret your joke as a command to be executed. Remember, your mind instructs your brain, and your brain instructs your body to become exactly what your mind believes!

Maui is a haughty, egotistical demigod from the movie *Moana*. He is known for his incredible shapeshifting abilities—a power granted to him by his magical fishing hook that he loses in the depths of the ocean. Upon reuniting with it, Maui struggles mentally with regaining his powers to shapeshift. Because of his insecurities, his mind doubts his ability to shapeshift. This doubt is relayed as a confusing and incoherent message to his brain, which in turn is relayed as a confusing and incoherent message to his body—so what happens? Maui shapeshifts into a disproportionate shark head with human feet—he looks ridiculous! But in time, and with encouragement from Moana, Maui quickly regains his confidence and begins shapeshifting like a pro.

Your mind is the author of your thought life, and it is the lens through which you experience your emotions. The thoughts and emotions you *choose* to think and feel, positive or negative, emit energy that converts into chemistry that affects your entire being. Your mind controls your brain, and your brain controls your heart, and your heart controls the growth medium of all the cells in your body. What is the growth medium? It's your blood! Bottom line, your thoughts and emotions impact each of the 50-plus trillion cells in your body.

The *rule of threes* states that you can go three weeks without food, three days without water, and three minutes without oxygen. Let's add a fourth fact—you CANNOT go three seconds without thinking and feeling—even in your sleep! Your thought life—brought to you by your mind—becomes your reality, and what you *choose* to think is up to you.

Who is the master?

Most people spend 95% of their lives on autopilot! That means our subconscious mind has stolen the show and our ability to live mindfully and in the moment. Again, we revisit the concept of the mind vs. the brain—but this time, we are pairing the brain and the body together. Which one is the master of your life? Why?

When we actively engage our mind and intentionally focus our attention, we are operating in the *cognitive control network*. We are fully aware and fully present in this state. Learning and retaining new information is done solely while operating in the *cognitive control network*. If we want to make positive changes in our life, we must activate this system. You probably already guessed it but if not, this program is run exclusively by your *mind*.

The subconscious mind operates on the *default mode network*—aka *autopilot*, and it encompasses our brain and our body. The fanciest Teslas use autopilot when driving their passengers around town. Sure, you may sit in the driver's seat, but the Tesla will do all the driving, and it is probably a safer driver than you and me! How does it do it? Well, it has all sorts of programs installed in it—from when to accelerate and decelerate, to turn, to stop, to switch lanes, etc. When we operate on autopilot, we are operating on old programs. Have you ever intended to drive to one location—let's say the mall—and then ended up somewhere else, like at work or at school? That's because your mind "spaced out" and your brain was on autopilot. At least your brain got you there in once piece! You have become so accustomed to doing various tasks that you don't need to think about the steps involved to accomplish them. While multi-tasking, we often go on autopilot for at least one of the tasks we are working to complete. Bottom line, you are *not fully aware* when you are on autopilot.

Autopilot runs all sorts of programs, from physical activities to psychological mindsets regarding how we relate to ourselves, others, and the world at large. The problem occurs when we go on autopilot and run dysfunctional or self-limiting programs that we downloaded early in life. For example, you can run a program grounded in a sense of being and feeling unworthy. Such programs can be destructive to our lives, especially if we are unaware of them. We will address the states of consciousness in chapter four. Autopilot is not bad. It is fantastic for conserving energy and allowing our mind to rest. However, we are not meant to spend most of our life in this state.

When we are operating on autopilot, our brain and body are the master over the mind, because the mind is in "sleep mode." Essentially, we lose our free will to the programs (physical and psychological) that we run while on autopilot. If we want to change our lives for the better, create and produce magnificent things, become the hero in our life journey, the mind must be the master to the brain and the body. Operating on autopilot is not living life to its fullest—it's simply going through the motions. Wake up! You have places to go, people to meet, and a world that needs what only you can offer!

Love and fear

In the 22nd century, humans are living on a luxurious starliner called the *Axiom*. It has orbited outer space for almost 700 years. Planet Earth has become a wasteland—mountainscapes have been replaced by garbagescapes. Consumerism, greed, and environmental neglect have made Earth uninhabitable. Buy N Large is a megacorporation whose unspoken mission is to make humans entirely dependent upon their products, technology, and ideology—a gluttonous lifestyle. Humans have become morbidly obese due to a loss in bone density and immobility. They no longer walk. Instead, they are transported via hover-loungers that project holographic images for communication and entertainment. Humanity has become stuck on autopilot since birth, completely unaware of their original home on planet Earth. Hundreds of years prior, the Buy N Large CEO instructed the passengers to "go on full autopilot—and do not return to Earth!" He convinced them that Earth's toxicity was lethal. Brainwashed by fear, humans became easily controlled and manipulated by Buy N Large's vicious agenda. What Disney movie evokes these dystopian vibes?

WALL-E is an extreme but also accurate portrayal of humanity, as most of us are stuck on programs, completely blind to the dysfunction they cause. If we are not careful, we lose our free will to programs. When trapped in the fear program, it is impossible to create to our fullest potential! Below are the two driving programs of humanity: fear and love. Which program are you operating on?

> *The chemistry of love enhances cell growth and vitality; while the chemistry of fear cancels it and even shuts down the immune system.—Dr. Bruce Lipton*

Fear

The Neuroscience of Fear: Survival instinct dictates that fear-related emotions, such as anger and anxiety, take priority over love-centric emotions. The average person spends approximately 70% of their life in a state of chronic stress. Essentially, stress can be perceived as a derivative of fear as it produces anxiety. Stress occurs when we evaluate our environmental demands as exceeding our ability to successfully cope with uncontrollable and unpredictable situations. Neurochemically, chronic stress produces and releases large amounts of adrenaline, noradrenaline, endorphins, and cortisol—the same chemicals produced by *fear.* This neurochemical cocktail helps us to run faster and fight harder when we are confronted with life-threatening circumstances. The emotion of fear triggers the fight or flight response (survival mode), and three things occur:

1.) The blood from the brain's frontal lobe (the problem-solving brain) is pumped into the limbic brain (primitive brain) to trigger the next steps of the fight or flight response.
2.) The limbic brain triggers the production of adrenaline, noradrenaline, endorphins, and cortisol, and disperses it

throughout the entire body via the bloodstream. These chemicals enhance your ability to fight or flee in life-threatening situations.

3.) To save our life, the blood rushes from the heart and the gut to the outer extremities to get us to move by running faster and fighting harder.

Fear in Perspective: Do you think that 70% of our experiences constitute a true threat to our survival? Certainly not. We live in a modern society of glass skyscrapers and superhighways, not in the Stone Age where predatory animals run rampant—so what do we fear? As a psychologist, I believe that the greatest human fear is failure in the context of relationships—failure to be enough—failure to connect— failure to perform—failure to achieve—failure to thrive—failure to love and to be loved. Fear is often disguised as anger, depression, self-loathing, insecurity, jealousy, obsession, perfectionism, and offense. We are originally wired for connection but fear wires us for protection. How ironic is it that we fear the failure to love? Love is the one thing that gives us wings to thrive and to flourish physically, spiritually, and psychologically.

This is a perfect example of the difference between the mind versus the brain. Your mind knows when a situation is a true threat to your survival. When a true threat is detected, your mind gives your brain full responsibility to manage what happens next. The brain is fantastic at responding quickly and efficiently. In a true survival situation, there is no time for the mind to overanalyze the threat and all the possible courses of action, along with their respective risk-benefit analysis. The brain has been known to do incredible feats during true fight or flight scenarios—almost like the Incredibles themselves. Yes, this includes lifting a vehicle to save a baby pinned underneath it!

In all instances, except those wherein your survival is truly in peril, your mind tells your brain what to fear and then the brain responds by producing the neurochemical cocktail of chaos (survival chemicals). How often do we visualize the worst-case scenario? Our imagination alone can trigger the survival response. Essentially, this is our mind telling our brain to produce the physical experience of "all things gone wrong!" This becomes an activity wherein we weaponize our very precious imagination and the incredible energy of our brain against ourselves. You may have heard FEAR as an acronym for FALSE, EVIDENCE, APPEARING, REAL. This is accurate for 99% of what we fear.

Please take note that fear is a powerful emotion, and it broadcasts a powerful electromagnetic signature. It is possible to manifest the fears you bring to life in your imagination by constantly thinking about them and allowing them to dictate your emotional state. Take Deepak Chopra's insight if you don't believe me: "The best use of imagination is creativity. The worst use of imagination is anxiety."

Prolonged fear: Operating on the fear program for extended periods of time negatively alters your *homeostasis*—otherwise known as your electrochemical balance. In fact, *allostasis* is the process by which your body responds to stressors and attempts to regain a functional and healthy homeostasis. However, remaining in a state of imbalance for too long can become the body's new norm.

Our dysfunctional and maladaptive subconscious programs tend to perpetuate and exacerbate our state of chronic stress. For example, believing that you are unworthy (subconscious program created in childhood) amplifies your fear of failure and your fear of rejection, which makes your daily activities more stressful. When this is our vibration (electromagnetic signature), we attract circumstances that match it and consequently reinforce it! Bad experiences result in the internalization of negative emotion, which may start off as "being in a funk." But over time that "funk" becomes a mood, and that mood becomes a temperament, and that temperament becomes a personality. As Dr. Joe Dispenza says, "Your personal reality becomes your personality." In this state, you don't see things how they are—you see things how YOU are. We become stuck in this "thinking-feeling-loop" that becomes increasingly more difficult to break free of.

Thinking feeling loop: What is a thinking-feeling-loop? It's a mind trap that keeps you stuck! When you start your day thinking about your problems, and those thoughts elicit a negative emotional state, that negative emotional state then results in negative behaviors, and such negative behaviors produce a negative experience, which in turn reinforces the negative thinking that started the nonsense in the first place. Think of the cute and cuddly lamb known as Lamp Chops—remember her annoying song? *It is the song that never ends, and it goes on and on my friends; some people started singing it, not knowing what it was, and then they kept on singing it forever just because...It is the song that never ends, and it goes on and on my friends, some people started singing it...* ALL RIGHT, ALL RIGHT ALREADY! Do you get the point? This repetition creates hardwired neural networks that are difficult to change. Again, we lose our free will to programs that we have created, and our today becomes a rerun of yesterday.

<u>Addicted to fear:</u> Here's the shocker: Your body becomes addicted to the electrochemical cocktail of chaos. Yes, just like a drug, your body desires this state of hyper-arousal! You become addicted to the neurochemicals of chronic stress, all the while you are attracting more negativity into your life because of the state of your electromagnetic signature. At this point, your electromagnetic signature is about as bright as an inanimate object. Your body has consumed all its energy to fight the perceived threat, which leaves you with no energy to restore and repair it. This results in your immune system being compromised. Moreover, there is an inverse relationship between *cortisol* (stress hormone) and *melatonin*—the body's natural sleep aid. The more stressed you are, the less sleep you get. There is no rest when you are activating your survival response. In this state, your body, which was once the servant, becomes the master of your mind as you navigate life on autopilot. If you're living by the same negative emotion every day, anchored emotionally to your past, your body is conditioned to this energy and state of being. It prevents your soul from creating anything new. Moreover, if you have the desire to make positive life changes, your mind is going to have to go into hand-to-hand combat with your body to regain its rightful position on the throne. That may be challenging since your mind does not have hands. All joking aside, when your mind is working to gain control of the body, the absence of the neurochemical cocktail of chaos can cause the body to experience cravings and withdrawals. The body will try and sucker the brain into creating the chemicals so that it can get its fix. If we are not aware, we will find ourselves being drama queens or kings because interpersonal friction is a quick way to stir up the electrochemical cocktail of chaos.

External joy: When in survival mode and stuck in a state of chronic stress, we are constantly bracing ourselves against our environment, the source of our perceived threat. We become so accustomed to allowing our environment to dictate our negative emotional state that we turn to the environment to also be our source of fulfillment. This results in retail therapy, lavish vacations, plastic surgery, drugs, a new sports car, and the list goes on.

Let's say you opt to take a ten-day Disney cruise to a tropical island to escape your chronic stress. The first three days are blissful because the experience is still new and frolicking with your favorite Disney characters has not yet gotten old. But as we reach vacation days 5-6, your body starts craving its electrochemical cocktail of chaos (stress chemicals), so you start creating problems to stir up this chemistry within your body. You may bicker with your spouse or get into a full-blown wrestling match with Minnie Mouse for no logical reason. Even though your external environment has changed while on a cruise, your brain will always believe its internal chemistry over its external conditions. No amount of Disney can fix this addiction—only you can. You must become aware of your behavior and redirect it.

Consuming pleasures from the environment produces a temporary "feel good" state. But when the "feel good" runs out, what happens? We search for more elevated environmental factors to take us back to "feeling good." Usually, we need more of the pleasure-producing stimuli than the time before, because the body builds a *tolerance* to it. Unfortunately, this results in new addictions that create larger and larger voids that must be filled. It's insatiable. Over an extended period, this creates a pattern of electrochemical chaos in our body that down-regulates our genes for premature death and disease. Essentially, you are operating like a thermometer, wherein the environment is constantly dictating your internal temperature. How do you counteract this?

Neurohacking fear: When you can identify yourself as trapped in the vicious cycle of seeking environmental stimuli to change your inner emotional state, you are at the brink of change. To regain your creativity, you need to shift out of autopilot and into an awakened state as you engage the *cognitive control network*—your conscious mind. It is here wherein we objectively explore what happens when we go on autopilot and identify the dysfunctional programs and patterns of our subconscious mind. These dysfunctional programs leave a path of destruction in our lives, and the best way to become aware of them is to examine the sort of destruction they leave behind. Allow the debris and wreckage to serve as clues that will eventually lead us to the root of our problem. This always requires us to swallow our pride and to be vulnerable, even if it means asking the people closest to us to point out our flaws.

When we identify the emotion(s) that is/are keeping us stuck, we work to free those emotions. When we do, we liberate the energy we used to attach ourselves to those emotions. Now we can take this energy back and use it to create something new—something in line with truth and love. At first, making the change is an uphill battle, as the body wants to reign as master over the mind, as it seeks to return to familiar electrochemical territory. But when one's intention to change is firm, the amplitude of that decision carries a level of energy greater than the hardwired programs of the subconscious mind and the body's emotional addiction. This powerful intention is motivated by the desire to break free from the dysfunction that is holding you back from living out your divine destiny! Remember, change always requires a mind and body experience—and as you know, thoughts are the vocabulary of the mind and emotions are the vocabulary of the body. To successfully change you must have a *dedicated decision* (thought) and a *fantastic feeling* (emotion) about it.

Once the negative energy harbored by the emotion that kept you stuck is set free, your personality begins to shift to a positive vibration that helps you to mend relationships and to attract new ones (healthy relationships). In this state, you begin to develop new programs that all fall in line with the *love program*. You once sought the environment to *cause* a positive *effect* on your inner emotional state; now you have evolved, and you become the cause to effect a positive change in your environment to attract the life your spirit desires. You were once the thermometer waiting on the temperature of the environment to change you but now you are the *thermostat* dictating the temperature of your environment. The stronger your positive emotional vibration the more influence you have over your material world. This is where creation begins! You have become the producer of your own happiness, as you no longer depend on substances, places, things, or people to make you happy. When you become aware of your automatic habits and behaviors, you will never become unaware of them again. You're so familiar with your pain and suffering that you will never allow yourself to return to that old emotional state. However, the best part is that you will learn how to train your brain and body to expect great things, which changes your personality, which then becomes your personal reality. Bottom line, you absolutely cannot create to your fullest potential when you are trapped in the fear program. It is the greatest hindrance between you and your divine design for your divine destiny.

◊ *Fear program in a nutshell:* In this program the body is the master to the mind. It operates on autopilot and is dictated by chronic stress, as well as our past negative life experiences that once triggered our survival response (fight, flight, freeze). Our negative emotions trigger the same thinking-feeling loop and the same experiences. We look to the environment as the source of all things—both fear and fulfillment. Like a thermometer, the temperature of the environment becomes the temperature of our inner emotional state. We fail to liberate negative emotional experiences of our past, which obscures our cognitive and emotional lens with negativity. This drains our energy. Our body becomes addicted to the electrochemical chaos caused by being stuck in chronic stress, stuck in the same thinking-feeling-loop, and being stuck on autopilot, which makes it even more challenging to break the vicious cycle. This compromises our immune system, depletes our energy resources, and dims our electromagnetic signature, which eventually down-regulates our genes for premature death and disease.

Love

We are neurobiologically wired to love and to be loved. Love requires relationship and relationship requires free will. Love is a choice. It is the most powerful and transformational form of energy in existence, and it is our deepest spiritual purpose and motivation. Love is greater than oneself and can only be discovered through connection and relationship.

Yes, you also have a relationship with yourself. How your mind speaks to your brain and body is real! It's called self-love. Do you have it?

My reference to love is in the broadest form—the need to connect, to trust, to be validated, to be accepted, to feel safe, to find comfort, to be free, to give-and-take, to share, to laugh, to bond, to explore, and the list goes on. Love is humanity's greatest driving force—we want it, and we need it so badly that we ironically tend to pour more energy into the fear of losing it than in love itself. The "poor little rich boy or girl" may possess all the material value that the world has to offer, yet they continue to feel empty if they don't have love.

Humans and other species capable of simply "getting along" with others have significantly improved potential for survival, reproduction, genetic fitness, and overall longevity. Positive relationships experience a complex set of life-promoting emotions that have come to be known as "love." Love has a multitude of definitions but let's examine the biobehavioral definition of love. It is the formation of *selective* connections that spawn a sense of *safety or trust* that encourage reproduction, and the enhanced ability to overcome fear, stress, and disease. The absence of love makes one vulnerable to neuroendocrine and autonomic dysfunction, as well as every sort of physical and emotional illness. Neurochemically, love effervesces *oxytocin* into the blood stream. It is a hormone that has anti-inflammatory and antioxidant properties (health promoting). In fact, oxytocin signals nitric oxide which signals endothelial derived relaxing factor, a chemical that prompts the arteries in your heart to literally expand. Love produces brain and heart coherence, which means that the rhythms of our mind and body are in sync. We often see "faith over fear" as a common phrase. Let me remind you that faith is a form of love. We use the term "love program" because it is more comprehensive and inclusive, as all good things derive from love.

◊ *Love program in a nutshell:* In this program the mind is the master to the body. This program operates in full conscious awareness (mindful), and you might even say that love is not a program, but for the purpose of learning let's refer to it as such. It is fully aware of its own functioning and can correct its course to live optimally in peace and harmony. In this program, you know how to neurohack the survival response when there is no imminent threat to harm. Through various means, this program transforms or expels negative energy (thoughts and emotions) in a timely manner. It is a program that thrives in order and harmony and up-regulates our genetic expression for health and longevity.

Disney perspective: Let's sprinkle a little Disney to drive the point home. In the movie *Monsters Inc.*, a monster is deemed a true hero the more terrifying they are to children. In fact, Monstropolis, the city in which they live, is powered by the screams of children. This is how it works: The monsters sneak into the children's bedrooms at night with the goal of making them scream in horror. The louder the scream, the more energy is harnessed to later power the city of Monstropolis. The children fear the monsters and the monsters fear the children even more. Monsters believe that children are toxic and lethal! Clearly, fear is the program driving this system.

Monstropolis is turned upside down when a little girl, affectionately named Boo, sneaks into their world through a bedroom door which serves as a portal between the two worlds. Initially, Sully and Mike (two monsters and main characters) are terrified of the toddler, until they come to recognize that she is sweet, funny, affectionate, and poses zero threat. During their interactions, they discover that making her laugh generates significantly more power than her nightmarish screams. Upon returning Boo safely to her home, not to mention all the chaos brought on by the villain (Randall), Monsters, Incorporated (the power plant) decides to make a big change. Children's laughter becomes the new source of "clean energy," as its power is far greater than their nightmarish screams. This new shift in priorities allows for monsters who were not talented "scarers" to have the opportunity to pursue standup comedy and become the new heroes of Monstropolis. This transition of deprogramming and reprogramming an old process is a bit painful, but it all works out in the end. Bottom line, love and laughter always wins!

There are two words that are the same length; both have identical letters but are arranged in a different order. Both words are grounded on opposite ends of the spectrum of life. Which one are you—the reactor or the *creator?*

Process Questions

- ➢ What brings me joy?
- ➢ What do I fear?
- ➢ Am I operating in a state of chronic stress?
- ➢ What emotions do I need to liberate?
- ➢ What interpersonal destruction have I caused?

  - ○ How do I behave?
  - ○ How do I feel?
  - ○ What are my thoughts when this happens?
  - ○ Do these thoughts belong to a subconscious program?

    - ▪ What is the program?
    - ▪ How did it form?
    - ▪ Does this program serve me?

- ➢ How have I demonstrated my courage?

Freedom Rhythm

- ➢ Please turn to page 180 to read about Freedom Rhythm and how to perform it.
- ➢ **Transformation Zone 3:**

  - ○ **Visualization with bilateral stimulation:** *I want you to recall all the courageous things you have ever done. Now, I want you to amplify that courage and imagine yourself doing new things!*
  - ○ The mindset that informs your creative movement:

    - ▪ Dedicated Decision: "I AM courageous."
    - ▪ Fantastic Feeling: "Courage and Strength."

  - ○ Creative movement: Now, put your experience into movement with your silk.
  - ○ Positive Affirmation: "I AM courageous! Yes, I AM!" x 3

Chapter 3

FLOW NOT FORCE

"The four C's of making dreams come true: Curiosity, Courage, Consistency, Confidence."

WALT DISNEY

Killing me slowly

MOMENT OF PERSONAL TRUTH: I despise talking about myself and even writing about myself. However, I believe there is incredible power in vulnerability, wherein lies the opportunity to connect and to inspire hope. Internalizing the testimonies of others has been the spark needed to ignite the flame of courage to transform my own life. I hope to demonstrate how living in love versus fear has radically changed who I am. Moreover, it has allowed me to flow harmoniously with the laws of the universe, even throughout hardship. I used to *force* things out of fear and need for control, but now, I *flow* as I trust in love to make the way. *Flow—not force.*

It's a no-brainer—pun intended—that we need to learn to override our survival instinct when it is not serving us. In the introduction of this book, I referenced a time in my life when I was operating in a state of chronic stress. As an Air Force Veteran and high-ranking government employee, I was responsible for the mental fitness for thousands of Soldiers across an installation. The demands were high and the access to mental healthcare was poor—add a splash of toxic leadership, maybe more like a tidal wave—and it was a recipe for disaster. Moreover, I was often discriminated against because of my demographics—a young Hispanic woman in a position of power that was typically held by a middle-aged Caucasian male. I have always been a driven whippersnapper, to say the least!

The straw broke the camel's back when I became a whistleblower to protect the Soldiers I served. Thereafter, I endured relentless retaliation from my chain of command. My heart sank into the pit of my stomach when I pulled up to work each morning. Every time my computer alerted me to a new email in my inbox, my heartrate skyrocketed and a sense of panic flooded me. I was completely and entirely operating in the fear program.

In the middle of the chaos, I took my family on that surprise vacation to Disneyland that I referred to in the Introduction of this book. I was very intentional about unleashing my inner child and leaving all the work stress behind. I couldn't help but think, *What is stopping me from living my life with this incredible sense of childlike wonder, fun, laughter, play, creativity, curiosity, and joy? Why can't I have this experience every day?* The magic ended when the wheels on the airplane hit the tarmac.

I was in survival mode every second of my working day. Even after five o'clock, I spent my evenings, nights, and weekends dreading my next work encounter. Was there something threatening my life? No—nothing at all—and yet my brain was responding to the orders of my mind as though there were a saber-tooth tiger roaming every square foot of my existence. What was I scared of? I was terrified of my very own definition of professional failure. Now, it's easy to judge me and to think, *This woman is ridiculous; her problems are nothing compared to…* Bottom line, everyone's emotional experience is their truth, and all hurtful situations are relative to their unique programming. Judging belongs to the *fear program*, which causes disconnect and disharmony, while acceptance allows us to connect and to grow with new insight in line with the *love program*.

During this chaos, I would pray for my nightmare to end—but it only seemed to get worse. I was confused. I was trapped in my own mind. I could not see clearly. You see, throughout my life there were very clear and evident steps of progression to get exactly where I wanted to go—from elementary school through my doctorate degree, to the rank-ordered structure of military and government service. I was climbing the ranks fast and furious—it was all I knew. I was stuck in a program that I created.

When I changed my prayer to "Divine intelligence that is love, lead me to a purposeful and meaningful calling that allows my spirit to soar—and at the same time, brings me peace and deep fulfillment," the answer came when I received an email from my leadership that quite literally blew my mind—it was so absurd that I laughed out loud. In that moment, I realized that it was *my choice* to tolerate professional bullying. Like a slap in the face, I quickly recognized that I was worthy of respect, dignity, and safety in my workplace.

During this time, a dear friend said to me, "You are like a baby bird in a very comfortable nest filled with your mothers' softest feathers. Those soft feathers are quickly being pulled from the nest, and it is making you increasingly more uncomfortable—and now it's painful—because you are not meant to stay in the nest. You are meant to soar!" The divine intelligence of love directed my friend to spontaneously give me the right message at the right time, so right then and there, I gathered all my evidence to fight the good fight for our Soldiers, sent my concerns to the General and then I resigned. It was time to soar!

During my time with the military, I was blessed to write the book *Peace After Combat*. It was something that my spirit urged me to do— to help our Service Members and their families find the healing they so much deserved. All that I had accomplished in this past life still had tremendous meaning and most importantly, I survived to tell the story. I am so blessed to have a supportive husband, also a veteran, who encouraged me to embark on the Hero's journey to discover my true spiritual calling that would someday become my legacy.

The first week after I resigned was amazing! I was barely wrapping my head around the idea of being free. Then, out of the blue, my body began craving the electrochemical cocktail of chaos produced by my brain while in survival mode. I began creating unnecessary drama with my husband to get my brain to produce the stress hormones all over again. I fell back into the fear program wherein my body was the master to my mind. In hindsight, I recognized that my husband went through the same type of withdrawal from chronic stress after retiring from the military after 26 years of service and multiple combat tours to Iraq and Afghanistan. It was time for me to neurohack my brain. I sought peace through prayer, exercise, meditation, and lots of dancing. I knew in my heart that there was a higher calling for my life to help humanity—much like the Japanese teaching of Ikigai—but I was not certain of how it would all play out.

Trust fall

Being a control freak was a characteristic that helped me to excel throughout my long and arduous academic career, and it also gave me a competitive edge when climbing the military ranks. I have always known that my calling is to teach people about the incredible power of their mind and how to harness it to live the life of their dreams. However, I didn't know the ins and outs of how I was going to get this message out to the world in a way that is unique to me. I was in search of my perfect self-expression. You see, each of us possesses a divine design for our divine destiny. However, we tend to dismiss it as "too good to be true" so it never manifests. How awful is that?

For the first time, I truly had to surrender the need for control and trust that the divine would make a way. I had to become what I wanted to attract. My *dedicated decision* was to spiritually surrender myself to receive the *answer* to my calling. When I say surrender, I don't mean "give up!" What I mean is that I am resisting the urge to control the outcome by allowing the divine to lead the way, as I humbly follow. My *fantastic feeling* was gratitude in anticipation for receiving the answer before its arrival. This is an act of faith and trust. The divine nature of love never disappoints, as it is the source of ultimate fulfillment.

There were distractions during this journey that would've threatened the outcome of my transformation if I had taken the bait. I had several government entities calling to hire me after my resignation, each one offering a higher rank and, of course, higher pay. The old me reveled gleefully at the flattery and wanted to say "yes" to each offer. It was so easy to fall back into the old and toxic cycle of chaos, all to be validated by the same beast. Had I said "yes" to those job offers, this moment—right now—you, reading this sentence of this book, would not exist. Moreover, I'd be back in the fear program, back to chronic stress, back to being a fish in the fishbowl. I had to intentionally neurohack my brain—to ensure my mind was master to my body. The Hero's journey is a journey of the spirit—not of the flesh.

If I went back to the program that almost killed me—just like a toxic relationship—I would never find my true calling—my purpose, my Ikigai. How did I know that this government work was not my true calling? Because I felt trapped (even when things went smoothly) and there was this relentless urge that whispered, *There is so much more…* It was like an itch that needed to be scratched, but nothing could relieve it—except that *one thing* I had yet to discover.

I filled this waiting period with things that I love—like art, décor, home renovation, teaching, and performance. Much of my time was spent volunteering in the community. I knew that the more I give, the more I get in return. If I wanted answers and open doors, I was going to have to sow good seed, to reap a good harvest, as the world of the generous gets larger and larger. This is the law of prosperity.

Back to the story: I felt inspired to partake in a competition that required talent. You guessed it: I decided to dance. Here's the thing: I used to be a professional ballet dancer in my late teens and early twenties. Being in my late thirties, I was not capable of dancing in the same way as I once did; it had been over a decade since I had choreographed a dance routine. I was rusty, to say the least. To make up for what I was lacking, I purchased a silk streamer in hopes that its beauty and flow would distract from my lack of technique. This silk streamer was a wider, shorter, and more colorful version of the ribbon traditionally used by rhythmic gymnasts. I was all set and ready to perform until I was informed of the bad press regarding the organization's operations. Triggered by the news, I withdrew from the competition. I was so bummed because I wholeheartedly looked forward to performing. I felt confused. In that moment, the death of my old life and my disappointment for an anticipated experience that would never happen hit me like a ton of bricks. Moreover, every unresolved emotion from past painful life events added to that weight—so what did I do? I blasted my music, and I projected all my pent-up hurt into movement with my silk streamer. Like a whip, I flung it around my living room, and like water gushing from a firehouse, I expelled all the toxic energy that lingered like poison in my veins. Liberating this energy was the last obstacle keeping me from my divine destiny. After this emotional purge, the clouds in my mind parted and the sunshine broke through—it was Freedom Rhythm: Emotion Focused Movement. I was to create a protocol to help people improve their physical and mental fitness by projecting their emotions through movement, with the use of vibrant and colorful silks. The silk would be the dancer and they would be the choreographer, as their movement would help to create a story to set them free! My life's mission sprouted out of a series of unfortunate events.

Freedom Rhythm: Emotion Focused Movement drew on my countless years of dance, my trauma and neuroscience expertise as a military psychologist, my writing, my love for music and performance, and my passion for all things fun and colorful. It was all the best parts of me rolled up into one. I have dedicated my life to many passions, often wondering if there was more to them than just the immediate gratification they were serving at that time. I imagine each of my passions as a colorful silk intertwining to create a beautiful braid. This is how the spirit of harmony works—no passion is ever in vain. I discovered perfect self-expression through my divine design for my divine destiny!

No one is immune to the pain and suffering of the world, but when you allow *love* to lead the way, it calls upon the *spirit of harmony* to create order out of disorder. When you allow fear to lead the way, harmony doesn't come to the rescue. More fear drives more chaos and more disorder. It was truly a trust fall to get to that point...

Whenever there is trust, there is faith! I have evidence that serves as proof that trusting in the divine nature of love works. It is the foundation of my faith—which is believing in the unseen before it is revealed. In college a couple of girlfriends and I had the wild idea to spontaneously drive to Disneyland from Texas, and we did it! We drove all throughout the night until we landed at the gates of Disneyland. Here's the thing: In the darkness of night, and when GPS did not exist, we had I-10 and headlights that cast light only ten feet in front of our vehicle. Even though we couldn't see farther than those ten feet, we had faith that the road would take us to our destination. That's how life is. You work with the knowledge you have in the moment and have faith that in the end it all works out—because it does.

Law of harmony

Every life experience is orchestrated through energy, frequency, and vibration. Your state of consciousness (thinking and feeling) determines your vibration, which attracts your three-dimensional experiences via the law of attraction. No one is immune to the pain and suffering of this world, but harmony will favor those who live in line with love. Harmony is like the flower that blooms in the rubble. It is the Phoenix rising from the ashes. Harmony provides balance and resolution amid chaos and disorder.

When you operate in the love program, harmony has a way of turning negative experiences into incredible opportunities. Harmony opens the new door when all the others have been slammed shut. However, harmony cannot come to the rescue when you are operating in the fear program, because there is no trust. While in the fear program, we are too busy trying to control everything to ensure that there are no unknowns, so we *force* situations. Harmony only has room to work when we *flow*... As you learned, fear evokes chaos and chaos in return evokes fear. *And we know that in all things the universe works for the good of those who love and who have been called according to its purpose (Romans 8:28).*

The Flow of Harmony basically means "trust in the universe;" it all works out. Personally, I think of harmony in the way that the myriad of pieces in a kaleidoscope, that are constantly shifting and transforming, all come together at exactly the right time and place to create symmetry and flow for a beautiful mosaic masterpiece. It is constantly moving, just like life. Sometimes we may look through the lens and not like the colors or shapes that we see, so we shake it until we are satisfied, and we fall into the rhythm and flow of its mesmerizing movement.

Love is a self-organizing intelligence that works hand-in-hand with the spirit of harmony. All chaos will eventually become organized by the spirit of harmony if we allow it. Most of us can agree that explosions create the ultimate kind of destruction—physical chaos. Let's rewind back to the Big Bang—the mother of all explosions. Now look at where we are now—even the law of nature surrenders to the law of harmony. All things will eventually work for the good of those who operate in the love program. After all, it's the law.

Law of non-resistance

You have undoubtedly heard the words, "what you resist persists." You've also read my phrase, "flow—not force." When we resist something, we are creating an opposing force that we will eventually struggle against, and the more we struggle against it, the more power we give it. Let's try it from another angle: When you willfully give your energy to what you resist, you end up feeding it, which results in it growing larger and more problematic. It's the exact thing that happened to me in my toxic work environment—the more energy I gave to the opposing force, the more it consumed me, sucking the life out of me just like a vampire. The sooner I stopped resisting it, the sooner it lost its power. If a person somehow becomes a problem in my life, I create an image of them in my mind and shower them with love and light. It's not always easy, but soon thereafter, the problem resolves itself with little or no effort on my end. Do not grant anyone or anything the power to steal your peace! Tao Te Ching's words are a perfect example of the law of non-resistance: "Nothing in the world is as soft and yielding as water. Yet for dissolving the hard and inflexible, nothing can surpass it. The soft overcomes the hard; the gentle overcomes the rigid. Everyone knows this is true, but few can put it into practice."

Laws of karma, forgiveness, freedom, grace, and prosperity

Law of karma: Remember, life is like a game of boomerangs. Every action we take and every thought we hold will come back to us—good or bad. The law of karma reasons that our actions have commensurate consequences that will manifest in due time. The law of karma contains the principles of the law of attraction. Sometimes we act in terrible ways, which means that the terrible energy that we projected outward will eventually find its way back to us—yikes!

Law of forgiveness: Thankfully, there is the law of forgiveness, by which we can cancel out the energy of our mistakes. As you guessed, this law is grounded in the love program. Asking for forgiveness is acknowledging that you did not abide by the rules of the love program and that your thoughts or actions were wrong. There is freedom in acknowledging your wrongdoings because you are allowing truth to prevail. Truth is what sets us free! It is a part of the love program and when the truth rings, freedom rings—and the tides miraculously begin to turn in our favor! The *law of freedom* states that the truth sets us free of all karma to act out the divine design for our divine destiny.

Law of grace: This is the best part: When you operate in the love program, you get access to several "Get Out of Jail Free" cards. This means that you don't get what you deserve—and this is a miraculous concept if you were a bad boy or bad girl! You get grace and favor over the law of karma. The law of grace is the unearned, undeserved, unmerited favor of divine love. See, it pays to operate in the love program!

Law of prosperity: The world of the generous gets larger and larger; the world of the stingy gets smaller and smaller. The one who blesses others is abundantly blessed; those who help others are helped (Proverbs 11:24-26). If you wish to expect wealth, prepare to give generously. Order is the law of prosperity. If your finances and your home are in disarray, do not expect to attract prosperity. There is a supply for every demand when we trust in the divine. Never ignore the urge or impulse to give; act upon it. When you do, the divine spirit of love uses you to bless others, as it will bless you. Give cheerfully and fearlessly, with great expectation. Do not hoard anything if you wish to attract prosperity. The *law of use* tells us that we should use the things we buy and then get rid of them or donate them. Keep everything in your life flowing—even your finances.

Law of faith

Faith is trusting in the laws of the universe that are grounded in love and truth to do exactly what they are meant to do. Essentially, it is believing in the unseen and trusting in the unknown as though it were already seen and known that everything you desire has manifested in your three-dimensional reality. As soon as you begin to doubt, you weaken your electromagnetic signature, which is the energetic bond between you and the universe—the direct line to manifestation. Casting all doubt and fear aside, you are creating this unseen future every day because you are constantly thinking and feeling—even in your sleep! When you identify your dedicated decision—*how you think*—and your fantastic feeling—*how you feel*—you are directly influencing your day-to-day experiences. These experiences then reinforce, validate, and confirm your original thinking and feeling, which brightens and strengthens your electromagnetic signature—drawing your ideal future closer to you each day.

You may think this is hokey and continue to minimize it with a rebuttal that may sound something like this: "It's all in our imagination—like our imaginary childhood friend—and hence, it has zero connection to our material world." But didn't we just discuss in-depth that our thoughts and feelings—a dedicated decision and a fantastic feeling, more specifically—create our material world? Our imagination is the medium used to create internally and externally. It is what makes us different than any other animal species. Imagination is a spiritual experience. You may believe that you are living in an objective, stagnant, and physical world—what it appears to be. However, this world is dynamic energy constantly moving and flowing in a way that our five senses cannot always detect.

Faith is an emotional experience that exists because of trust—both of which produce peace. Trust is a mandatory prerequisite for faith. You must have faith in what you imagine for it to take a physical form.

If you have no faith in its possibility to exist, you would not waste your time to create it—and hence, it will not exist (because you didn't have faith in it to begin with). Don't forget, your brain does not know the difference between a real and an imagined experience, because an imagined experience has the same potential as a lived experience. Your imagination is the soil that grows your dreams into reality. As Albert Einstein says, "Imagination is the preview to life's coming attractions!"

When we believe and see it in our imagination, we become it and receive it in our 3D reality. Faith is believing and speaking that your dreams will come true—if they are in line with truth and love. Imagine—pun intended—that you are waiting for a package to be delivered to your home. It is something that you have wanted so badly for as long as you can remember. The delivery address is on Faith Street—good thing, because you have *faith* that you will indeed receive the package. However, after a few days pass and you haven't received the package, you begin to doubt that the package will arrive. In your doubting, you leave Faith Street, and you go down Uncertainty Lane searching for it, and then you continue down Doubtful Drive, and nothing! All the while, your package was delivered to Faith Street, while you were too busy searching for it on Uncertainty Lane. This package is the kind of package that requires your signature—it is too precious to be left at the doorstep. You lost your chance in that moment.

Faith requires discipline and patience. All too often, we rush what we desire to see manifest in our lives. This results in force—and as you know, force is driven by fear and a lack of faith. Force occurs when we become impatient with faith and choose to override the superpower of the law of attraction and take matters into our own hands. What we produce in the absence of faith is only a shadow of its fullest potential. Sometimes it is so hard to trust in the divine timing of the Universe that we start to lose our faith, and as a result, we miss our blessing. The divine knows the perfect time for everything, including the perfect time to begin the unfolding of your hopes and dreams.

This is an odd comparison, but I believe that it will convey my point. Imagine that you are so excited to have a baby and you just discovered that you or your partner is pregnant! You have been waiting for this moment for as long as you can imagine. You believe that you were ready for a baby many years ago. Impatient to see your baby, you decide to expedite the process and *force* the baby out prematurely at 28 weeks (no doctor would do this—it's just an example). Now, your baby is incubating in a glass bubble with tubes attached to its body. It is barely surviving. If it does survive, your baby will have to live with all sorts of complications that will significantly reduce its quality of life. Just because you were ready to have a baby years ago doesn't mean that your baby was ready for you!!!

Your hopes and dreams are like your baby. Do not prematurely deliver your hopes and dreams because of your impatience. Sometimes your dreams may be ready, but you are not. If you receive your dream before you are ready, you may unintentionally sabotage it. Remember, *flow* and not force! This is one of the many reasons why the serenity prayer exists: "Divine, grant me the serenity to accept the things I cannot change, the courage to change the things I can, and the wisdom to know the difference."

Truly, I find the greatest comfort in knowing that when I surrender to the incredible power of divine love, I will not miss what is meant for me—even when I mess up! The power of love is abundant in grace, granting us unearned, undeserved, and unmerited favor. We are often gifted with second and third chances to get our lives right—never take that for granted.

When the divine spirit of wisdom introduces a fantastic idea to your imagination—pursue it! Starting the process of creation can be a challenge. Do not be overwhelmed with "how" to immediately bring your idea to completion—just start. Too often, we discourage ourselves from starting because we don't know how or where to begin. The "how to" is not up to you—it's up to the divine spirit of wisdom to guide you. You must be willing to do the work and keep the faith that the right guidance will be revealed at the right time. When you ask for divine guidance—it will appear. Quit discouraging yourself from starting because you don't know "how!" Take a leap of faith and start creating—after all, it is what you were born to do!

Therefore, I tell you, whatever you ask for in prayer, believe that you have received it, and it will be yours (Mark 11:24).

Process Questions

- ➢ What experiences do you have with divine love?
- ➢ What are you resisting that is likely persisting in your life?
- ➢ How do you need to change your prayer or meditation to manifest what you want?
- ➢ What do you feel you are forcing in your life?
- ➢ How have you seen the spirit of harmony work in your favor?
- ➢ How has the law of grace played out in your life? Is there anything that you received that you felt was exceedingly abundant?
- ➢ What are your passions?
- ➢ What might be obstructing the revelation of your divine design for your divine destiny?
- ➢ Is there anything preventing you from trusting and having faith in the divine spirit of love?

  - o If so, what is it? How can you overcome it?

Freedom Rhythm

- ➢ Please turn to page 180 to read about Freedom Rhythm and how to perform it.
- ➢ **Transformation Zone 3:**

  - o **Visualization with bilateral stimulation:** You must remain on Faith Street because that is the delivery address for the blessing you've been waiting for…It is delivered at the proper time—when you are spiritually mature enough to handle it! Your blessing will blow your mind. Impatience leads to anxiety and doubt. These emotions cause you to drift to the wrong streets, some darker than others. Keep working your dreams and the breakthrough will come!
  - o *I want you to visualize remaining on Faith Street despite the urge to move—and receive the blessing at the perfect time.*

o The mindset that informs your creative movement:

- Dedicated Decision: "I have faith!"
- Fantastic Feeling: "Gratitude."

o Creative movement: Now, put your experience into movement with your silk.

o Positive Affirmation: "I AM faithful. Yes, I AM!" x 3

PART III: DEATH & REBIRTH

Illustration of
John Campbell's
Hero's Journey

Call to
Adventure

Supernatural
aid

Return

Known

Unknown

Threshold
(beginning of
transformation)

Atonement

The Hero's

Mentor

Helper

Challenges and Temptations

Journey

Transformation REVELATION

Death &
Rebirth

Helper

Chapter 4

THE MOST POWERFUL
TWO WORDS

"The more you like yourself, the less you are like anyone else, which makes you unique."

WALT DISNEY

I AM vs. "I'm"

WHO ARE YOU? OR WHO do you believe you are? Are you awesome, powerful, brilliant, and an overall worthy person? Or are you sad, miserable, negative, and an overall unworthy person? Are you looking for your next big break to be the source of your happiness? Or are you the source of your own happiness? How you opted to answer those questions is correct! You are whoever you believe you are, and your physical reality reflects your beliefs. As Stephen Covey says, "You don't see the world as it is; you see it according to who you are." Let's try it from another angle: *For as a person thinketh in their heart, so are they (Proverbs 23:7).*

There are two types of "I am." The first is the true "I AM." This is your superconscious mind and your truest identity. It is infinite and unlimited. It contains your divine design for your divine destiny. Florence Scovel Shinn describes it: "There is a place that you are to fill and no one else can fill, something you are to do, which no one else can do." You are both the creation and the creator. You are energetically connected to all of time and space and to every living thing. "I AM" is your spirit—your authentic self, grounded deeply and profoundly in both love and truth. This is your *original* programming, aka the *love program*. It promotes connection, a limitless mindset, as well as peace and order. For the purpose of this book your true "I AM" will always be presented in all capital letters. The other is a shadow of the phrase "I AM" and will be addressed as the contraction "I'm" in lower-case letters.

"I'm" is how YOU define yourself. It includes all the beliefs of the world—good and bad—integrated into it. Unfortunately, for most of us, the *fear program* aka the "worldly program" has neuro-hijacked our *love program*, stealing our I AM and swapping it for the lesser version, "I'm." The *fear program* promotes disconnect, a limited mindset, as well as chaos and disorder. When your divine destiny flashes across your conscious awareness, the fear program dismisses the vision as an unattainable ideal and chalks it up as "too good to be true," so it never manifests. We become like automatons when operating in the *fear program*, which makes it easier for us to be controlled by a more dominant force. The most oppressive lie programed into our subconscious mind is, *I'm NOT enough*. Our objective is to revert our "I'm" back to our "I AM" until we have only one identity—"I AM." It is our I AM that has VIP access to the universe to fulfill our heart's desires through manifestation. We lose our VIP access to the universe when our "I AM" is forced to stand in the shadows of "I'm."

Let's call on Disney to demonstrate this for us! My all-time favorite Disney character is Judy Hopps from the movie *Zootopia*. This is a movie about perseverance and overcoming negative stereotypes that cause destruction through division. Zootopia is a mammal metropolis wherein predator and prey live together in "harmony." Against all odds, Judy Hopps paid with blood, sweat, and tears to become the first rabbit to join the police force. Determined to prove herself worthy of the badge, she jumps on the city's most shocking unsolved mystery. Unexpectedly, Nick Wilde, a "sly and cunning" fox with a criminal record, crosses her path. Later, Judy discovers that his criminal mentality and networking capabilities will help her to solve the case. The two are like water and oil—criminal and cop—predator and prey. If Judy has any shot at cracking the case, she and Nick must learn how to work together. This requires them to partake in deep self-introspection to heal from past childhood trauma caused by bullying and negative stereotyping.

Nick Wilde has a heartfelt moment wherein he explains to Judy "why he is the way he is." He describes a traumatic story that takes place at approximately the age of eight. Nick wants nothing more than to become a part of the "pack" in the Zootopia Junior Ranger Scouts. Nick is lured down into a basement by the "pack" of children who identify as prey. Nick recites the creed: "I, Nicholas Wilde, promise to be brave, loyal, helpful, and trustworthy!" Afterward he is pinned down by the pack. Nick cries out in fear, "What did I do wrong?" The leader responds, "If you thought we would ever trust a fox without a muzzle, you're even more ignorant than you look!" They fasten a muzzle around his snout and kick him out of the house and into the streets. After reflecting on this painful event, Nick tells Judy, "I learned two things that day. One: I was never gonna let anyone see that they got to me." Judy replies, "And two?" Nick continues, "If the world is only gonna see a fox as shifty and untrustworthy, there's no point in trying to be anything else." Nick lost hope after this childhood trauma and henceforth allowed the world to define him by a negative stereotype rooted in the *fear program.*

Nick decided that life would be "less disappointing" if he lived up to the stereotype of the fox—sly, cunning, and untrustworthy. He was discriminated against on a regular basis, so he made no attempt to fight the stereotype. Nick chose to take a passive stance when determining his identity, and he allowed the fear program to define him. After all, Nick feared rejection above all else.

Oddly, Judy was bullied by predators for her desire to become part of the Zootopia Police Department. Moreover, her parents worked tirelessly to discourage her from chasing such an "unrealistic dream" and instead urged her to become a carrot farmer in Bunny Burrow. Her father told her, "See? That's the beauty of complacency, Judy. If you don't try anything new, you'll never fail!" Judy is truly unique, as she did not cave to the pressures of her parents and the stereotype of the world deeply rooted in the *fear program*. Instead, she was determined to prove everyone wrong about their perception of "bunnies" only being good for multiplying, cuteness, and carrot farming.

Before embarking upon a new and unknown experience, Judy states, "There's nothing to fear but fear itself." She has a courageous spirit grounded solidly in the *love program*. She is one-of-a-kind as she works diligently to fight an uphill battle to shatter the glass ceiling. Eventually, Judy inspires Nick to heal from the hurt of his past and to embrace his tender heart so that he can become kind and trustworthy—his true self. The unconditional love provided by Judy's friendship gave Nick the courage to break the mold and become the first fox to graduate from Zootopia's Police Academy. Judy is not left empty-handed for all the battles she fought. Foremost, she broke the glass ceiling after cracking the city's most jarring unsolved mystery and instantly became the most popular and most respected officer on the Zootopia Police Force.

No matter your circumstances, your "I AM" has always existed—and has always been waiting for you to believe it and become it. It is your "I AM" that is inextricably connected to the universe and works as the intermediary for manifestation. Judy believed through and through that she was a police officer even before she ever became one. In fact, she portrayed a police officer in a school play and giddily pranced around in a costume uniform. Even when she was bullied for her beliefs as a child, she sought justice via honorable measures and continued to embody the spirit of an upright police officer. Judy's "I AM" did not have to compete with "I'm." At the right time, her internal "I AM" became her 3D experience in the material world. Wait, is it 1D or 2D because she's a cartoon?! Oh my! You get the point.

In contrast, Nick Wilde chose to allow the world to determine his identity for him—a negative identity rooted in fear. His "I AM" waited patiently in the shadow of his "I'm," which was grounded in the world's beliefs about a sly fox. However, as a child, Nick's true spirit, his "I AM," was aligned with the creed that he so passionately took, "to be brave, loyal, helpful, and trustworthy." To protect his heart, Nick created an inflexible identity rooted in a pejorative stereotype. Nick became exactly who he believed himself to be—a sly fox with a criminal record. His "I'm" became his reality. Casting a shadow over your "I AM" interferes with your electromagnetic signature's broadcast, which prevents your divine design from manifesting.

We must applaud Nick for not allowing his "I'm" to continue to write the story of his life and block the glory of his "I AM." He had the courage to be vulnerable to a new way of life. Nick allowed himself to experience the emotions of acceptance and validation through love, allowing his I AM to outshine his "I'm." Nick courageously chose to make his "I AM" his only identity—no matter how incongruent it was with the rigid and inflexible thinking of the world who inherently feared predators.

The life you are living today is because of the person you decided to become and the beliefs you chose to internalize. Your claims decree reality. The best part is that everything can shift instantly—if you decide it to be so and act in accordance with your decision. Let's drive this point home: Your "I AM" is the real you grounded in love and truth. It is courageous, joyful, kind, trustworthy, loyal, lovable, powerful, brilliant, faithful, harmonious, peaceful, genuine, and so on and so forth. Are you like Nick? Did you have to hide your "I AM" to fit in with the world around you? Did you do it to protect yourself? Did you have to dim your light so that others wouldn't feel threatened by the power of your "I AM?"

Living incongruently with your true self results in *cognitive dissonance.* This is when you behave in ways that are incongruent with how you think. Cognitive dissonance causes anxiety. If we are stuck on behaving in a certain way, we work to change our thoughts to accept our behaviors. Essentially, we start rationalizing the behavior even when we know it is wrong. Nick's true self ("I AM") is loyal and trustworthy, yet he chose to act like a sly and cunning fox because that is what the world expected of him—it was easier to go with the flow of the stereotype. This resulted in spiritual and psychological incongruence that forced Nick to choose "I'm" (who the world believed him to be) over his "I AM." Now, his beliefs about himself were congruent with his behaviors and the world's beliefs about him. Here's the big problem: Living unfaithfully to your "I AM" has dire consequences that eventually lead to disease and premature death. We will discuss the biological underpinnings of epigenetics in the pages to come.

Just like Nick, it's never too late to live congruent with your "I AM." This is the part in the Hero's journey wherein you experience the death of your old self ("I'm") that was formed by the *fear program* and instead, you choose to be reborn of your original creation with perfect self-expression—your true self—your spiritual-self—operated by the *love program*. Expand your self-concept wherein your current self and your spiritual-self become one. Through your imagination, explore the emotional experience of this new and improved version of you. This is the part wherein you state your *dedicated decision*—"to become my 'I AM' (be specific)"—and your *fantastic feeling* to match this intention. Just like Judy, when you operate in the belief that you've already become this version of you, you become it, and you attract all the magnificence that comes with it.

Remember, you cannot attract what you are not! It's more than just self-talk. It's cute to think that you can repeatedly tell yourself that you are rich and hope to become rich. But if you believe you are poor, and you're merely reciting the words "I am rich," your desire will not manifest. First off, let's define rich as abundant and prosperous. If you want to be rich, your personality must become rich—through and through. Be patient because it takes time to neurobiologically deprogram the old mindset and program the new mindset. Once you allow all your negative self-beliefs to fall away, until all that exists is your "I AM," the only option is to attract all your heart's desires because it is the law. When you embrace your "I AM," your personality becomes your personal reality. Bottom line, become the energy that you desire to attract.

Law of intuition

Intuition is the perfect guide, and it comes from your superconscious mind, the home of your "I AM." Sometimes we call it a hunch. It's a strong feeling in the center of our chest that often pulls us like a magnetic force to do something for our benefit. Many people have failed to follow their intuition and have found themselves in precarious situations. Intuition is not only a means of protection to guide you out of harm's way, but it is also a navigator that points you closer to your divine design so that you may experience your perfect self-expression. All you must do is ask the divine spirit of love within you to lead the way. Be patient and keep your eyes open to its direction. It will show you signs that speak uniquely to you. Those signs will either affirm the direction you are on, or they will cause you to pause and slow down. Don't be frustrated with intuition, as it is a spiritual power that points the way but fails to explain how or why. In the Hero's journey, intuition is identified as the supernatural aid that guides you into the great unknown. Remember, creation of any kind is an adventure of epic proportions. It's time now to deprogram your "I'm" and reprogram your "I AM," because you were born to create!

Process Questions

➤ List the positive self-affirmations that you need to practice the most.

➤ What limiting self-beliefs do you need to deprogram?

➤ What is blocking your "I AM?"

➤ Did you have to hide your "I AM" to fit in with the world around you?

○ Did you do it to protect yourself?

○ Did you have to dim your light so that others wouldn't feel threatened by the power of your "I AM?"

➤ List everything you have accomplished that you are proud of—big or small.

➤ How has your intuition helped you?

Freedom Rhythm

➤ Please turn to page 180 to read about Freedom Rhythm and how to perform it.

➤ **Transformation Zone 3:**

○ **Visualization with bilateral stimulation:** *I want you to visualize your negative self-beliefs written on a sheet of paper, and I want you to destroy them. Now, I want you to visualize your positive self-beliefs growing larger and larger.*

○ The mindset that informs your creative movement:

▪ Dedicated Decision: "I AM limitless!"
▪ Fantastic Feeling: "Excitement and eager anticipation."

○ Creative movement: Now, put your experience into movement with your silk.

○ Positive Affirmation: "I AM limitless. Yes, I AM!" x 3

Chapter 5

KNOW YOUR KINGDOM

"The greatest moments in life are not
concerned with selfish achievements
but rather with the things we do for
the people we love and esteem."

WALT DISNEY

Ruling your kingdom

THE CAMERA FOLLOWS TINKERBELL'S STAR-DUSTED flight across a placid lake reflecting the twilight sky, just past a steaming locomotive rushing across a bridge, and beyond the lush, green, beautiful landscape. Her journey continues up a powerful and exhilarating waterfall and finally around the magnificent, blue-spindled Cinderella's castle that is lit by a rainbow of fireworks. The camera pans out, depicting the landscape of the kingdom, from the Matterhorn to Pride Rock. The sky is a delicious swirl of pink, purple, blue, and orange. For the grand finale, Tinkerbelle lights a sparkling fairy dusted trail across the tops of the castle and the words "Disney: 100 Years of Wonder" appear, signifying the beginning of yet another Hero's journey.

Many Disney movies portray a magnificent kingdom with a

beautiful castle at the top of a hill. Pick your favorite Disney castle and imagine that every inch of it belongs to you. Your castle has three primary levels. In descending order is the high tower that is perched just above the balcony, followed by the storehouse at the ground level, and the underground dungeon. As the ruler you reside at the balcony level because it offers you an incredible panoramic view of your majestic kingdom while providing easy access in and out of the castle. When you wish to leave your lavish abode, you must pass through the storehouse at ground level. As the hero in your story, there is never a reason to visit the dungeon.

The superconscious mind: Your powerful potential exists in the high tower—your superconscious mind. Recall that this is where your divine design for your divine destiny is housed. Each one of us, has something totally unique to offer the world that will bring us supreme satisfaction, as it is our form of perfect self-expression. The world needs this unique gift that only you possess. Unfortunately, our conscious awareness tends to reject it as too idealistic and impossible to achieve so it is dismissed as child's play. We don't dare to dream that big because we fear that it will end in failure and disappointment. Do you think that Walt Disney limited his superconscious mind?

The conscious mind: If your mind is not wandering, your conscious awareness is where you are residing right now as you read this sentence. Relative to your castle, your conscious awareness is the sprawling balcony to which both the high tower of your superconscious mind and the storehouse of your subconscious mind are attached. This state of mind lives in the present and nowhere else. When you are aware of your internal and external experiences, you are living in the now—the mindful moment. The conscious mind is the portal to neurohacking the dysfunctional programs embedded in your subconscious mind. It is the conscious awareness that chooses which programs to run. Hopefully, you have the courage to run the programs of your superconscious mind that contain your divine design. Running old and unhealthy programs of the subconscious mind limits your powerful potential. The only way to eliminate these dysfunctional programs is to become *consciously aware* of them. Deepak Chopra says it best: "Consciousness is infinite; and therefore, it has infinite gifts to give."

The subconscious mind: Your subconscious mind is a part of your consciousness, just as the balcony is connected to the storehouse of your castle. The subconscious mind is the part of the conscious mind that is not presently in focal awareness. Like a storehouse, the subconscious mind collects memories of all experiences, interactions, and impressions that create the programs you run when you go on autopilot. Think about it: Your brain and body keep a score of all your emotional experiences. Your brain and body have triggers that were conditioned during emotional highs and lows. Tension headaches, accelerated heartrate, back pain, and an upset stomach are all clues to how your subconscious mind is programmed. In fact, your subconscious mind is the key to your physical health, as we spend most of our time in this state of being.

To operate in the conscious mind, you cannot be on autopilot, running old programs from the storehouse. Some of these programs may be dysfunctional, which negatively affects the castle and the surrounding kingdom—and the worst part is that you are not aware of it! Your subconscious mind leaves metaphorical breadcrumbs or clues about its programming. When your subconscious programming is dysfunctional, it leaves a path of destruction behind it. If we care about improving ourselves, we will examine this path of destruction and identify the patterns of behavior that created it. Then we must become curious about the thoughts that preceded those behaviors to determine the source of the program. Is your brain on fire yet?

Most of our programs, good and bad, were created when our brain was the most neuroplastic—between zero and eight years of age. Recall that this was the critical period in Nick Wilde's life wherein he was bullied and consequently traumatized. His dysfunctional programming began early in his life. Deprogramming old and maladaptive programs and replacing them with new ones is the process of neurohacking. Basically, we are deleting the brain's old and dysfunctional neural networks that keep us stuck and instead, we are creating new neural networks by internalizing thoughts, emotions, and behaviors that are congruent with the future we wish to create.

Ironically, the world tends to associate mindfulness with meditation. Meditation is the least mindful process you will encounter, as it requires you to slow down your brain waves, and in doing so, you access your subconscious mind. The subconscious mind is fantastic for conserving energy, but we are not meant to spend most of our lives in this state. In fact, the subconscious mind uses 10-60 microvolts squared of energy, while the awakened conscious mind uses *a million microvolts* of energy. Wake up!

All new subconscious programs start in our conscious awareness. Whether we rehearse a mantra to aid in a new and adaptive way of thinking, intentionally shift our emotional state, or try something new, we must do it in a mindful and conscientious manner. Over time, when a new skill (thinking, feeling, or behaving) is practiced repeatedly, it becomes second nature—or automatic. This is when the neural network is strong enough to be performed on autopilot as a program of the subconscious mind. This mind-blowing process is called learning.

Truly, you become limitless when you program your subconscious mind with the thoughts of the superconscious mind. Flooding the subconscious with the ideas of the superconscious makes us one with the divine spirit with in us—"I AM!" Moreover, we can only receive what we see ourselves receiving. You cannot give or receive more than your subconscious mind believes is possible. This is the *law of expectancy and limitation*. According to Florence Scovel Shinn, "You are bound only by the limiting expectancies of the subconscious."

The unconscious mind: Much like the dungeon that we do not access while residing in our castle, our unconscious mind is detached from any part of our consciousness. The unconscious mind is a series of programs that occur automatically and are not available to self-introspection. They include programs that are made up of thoughts, memories, and primitive or instinctual desires that are buried deep within us; yet unbeknownst to us, they have an influence on our behavior. When we positively alter the subconscious mind, it will have a positive effect on the unconscious mind, as everything is interconnected.

Are the wheels in your head turning? Are you thinking about what lies beneath the surface of your thoughts, emotions, and behaviors? The states of consciousness are just like the iceberg that wrecked the Titanic. We only see the portion of the iceberg that is above the water, often underestimating the vastness of what lies beneath the surface. It is the part that we don't see that causes the shipwreck. Programs formed from love and truth (love program) create the foundation on which to build expansive and everlasting empires, while programs formed from deceit and fear create a foundation that will quickly fumble and crumble. Get curious and stay curious about why you are the way you are. But most importantly, have the courage to change "for you, and for me, and the entire human race. There are people dying; if you care enough for the living, make a better place for you and for me..." Oops! My autopilot took over and I started typing and humming the lyrics to *Heal the World* by Michael Jackson. You got me!

Family attachment

Disney's movie *Encanto* is about a family who faced tragedy and misfortune but was blessed with an everlasting miracle because of it. An armed conflict forces Alma Madrigal, her husband and their three babies to flee their home village in Colombia. While protecting his family in the armed conflict, Alma's husband is killed right before her eyes, but her candle magically repels the attackers from harming her and her children. The magic of the candle creates a beautiful casita, a sentient house for the family to live in. Encanto is in an enchanted realm bordered by high mountains. Fifty years later, Alma's children and grandchildren are given "magical talents or gifts" by the candle— all but Mirabel. The Madrigal family uses their magical talents to help their small village to thrive and prosper under the candle's protection.

Mirabel is discouraged because she is not magically gifted like the rest of her family. She and her Uncle Bruno are the family outcasts. The family fears Bruno because he was gifted with the ability to see into the future. When he informed the family and villagers of unpleasant visions of the future they began to fear him, falsely believing that Bruno was the cause of the misfortune. Bruno spoke the truth about his visions, but instead of using his gifts as an advantage, his family feared and shunned him. In fact, a famous catchy melody and lyrics were written about him: "We don't talk about Bruno, no, no, no..." Are you seeing evidence of the *fear program* yet?

Alma, the matriarch, pushed her family to be the very best and often expressed her disappointment in Mirabel's lack of gifting. When things went wrong in the household, Alma made it a habit to blame Mirabel by manipulating the situation. Mirabel's legitimate concerns about the magic of the casita being in peril were gaslit (dismissed/manipulated) by her grandmother. Mirabel was sensitive to the energy in the home, and she recognized that her family was struggling to "be perfect" in the unique areas in which they were gifted. With all the pressure from Alma, the family members did not feel "good enough" to meet her high standards.

After many attempts by Mirabel to help heal the "brokenness" of her family, the casita finally collapses, and the family loses their magical gifts in the middle of an argument between Alma and Mirabel. It is in this moment that Mirabel has the courage to speak the truth about Alma's negative influence over the family. Mirabel's words resonate deeply and profoundly within Alma. Mirabel then visits the location where Alma watched her husband die decades earlier. There, she sees a vision—a young version of Alma overcome with grief and fear of the future. Mirabel now understands that Alma was always operating in fear, terrified that the magic would vanish if her family was not perfect. Losing the magic meant that Alma would be stranded and alone, just as she was when her husband died. Alma sacrificed the emotional wellbeing of herself and her family to strive for perfection to keep the magic alive. Her belief about how and why the magic worked was wrong.

Alma sincerely apologizes to Mirabel, who now sees Alma from a new and compassionate perspective that she had never considered. Together, the entire family, the village, and the long-lost brother Bruno rebuild the casita. Mirabel's magical gift becomes evident when she unlocks the power of the candle over the home and her family once more. Mirabel is in line to become the next matriarch to lead the family from a place of love and not fear. In the end, it is evident that the magic did not seek perfection. Instead, the magic is, and was always, *love*. Love provides a safe place for everyone to experience and cultivate their unique gifts in a harmonious way, embracing their perfect imperfections.

Alama's traumatic history was the reason she chose to lead with fear over love. The way she chose to treat her family, especially Mirabel, was done from a place of apprehension. She feared that if she and her family were not good enough, the magic would run out and she would have to relive the same tragedy that she experienced decades prior. If Alma had the courage to be vulnerable sooner and had chosen to listen with an open heart to Mirabel's insights, the casita would have not collapsed. Too often, it takes an outpouring of destruction within our lives to get our attention to make change. We need to swallow our pride and seek the truth—even if it hurts—to avoid our own demise before it's too late. *Offense* is typically the greatest obstacle to truth. It is accurate to say that the truth will set you free, but there's no guarantee that the truth will be easy to receive.

Alma operated in the *fear program*. She shaped how her children and grandchildren viewed themselves, others, and the world at large. Alma's family also downloaded her fear program into their minds, more specifically as it related to "perfection as the only option." Additionally, they internalized an attitude of unworthiness, as they "would never be enough." When perfection is the only option, no one will ever measure up! Remember, fear wires us for protection over connection. Because Alma and her family internalized beliefs rooted in fear, they became increasingly more disconnected from one another. The more disconnected they became, the more the magic faded. Remember the law of attraction? How they felt internally manifested in their physical world and resulted in the crumbling of their casita and the loss of their magical gifts. But thank goodness for the laws of forgiveness, grace, and harmony—Alma got a second chance because she embraced the truth, and she allowed love to win!

In contrast, Mirabel led with love the entire time. She had moments of self-doubt, but she never succumbed to them. Mirabel allowed her intuition to guide her. She demanded to learn the truth—no matter how terrifying it was. Mirabel was not too prideful to consider the idea that the destruction of the casita was because of her lack of gifting, even though this was not the case. The rest of her family, especially Alma, lived in denial and refused to speak about the negativity they all were experiencing. The façade of perfection became more important than the foundation of truth and love.

Mirabel's mother possessed the magical gift of physical healing, while Mirabel was gifted in spiritual healing. The Madrigals' new home was built on a foundation of love and truth vs. a foundation of fear that presented itself as perfection. Never build your casita, kingdom, empire, or your *mojo dojo casa house* on a foundation of fear, as it is only a matter of time before it collapses.

Program formation

> *"If you feel safe and loved, your brain becomes specialized in exploration, play, and cooperation; If you are frightened and unwanted, it specializes in managing feelings of fear and abandonment."* Dr. Bessel van der Kolk

From birth to the age of eight, your brain creates programs that dictate how to relate to the world. We have special brain cells, called *mirror neurons*, that are responsible for learning through imitation. They play a key role in how we interact in relationships, helping us to interpret all aspects of emotion, from body language to facial expressions. Mirror neurons contribute significantly to the formation of the programs that often dictate the outcomes of our relationships. Don't forget, ninety-five percent of our behaviors are dictated by our subconscious mind—our autopilot.

During the critical developmental periods of childhood, we observe the interpersonal exchanges of our primary caregivers, and their interactions with us become the relational template we use throughout life—good, bad, or ugly. These interactions dictate how we view ourselves, others, and the world at large. It is obvious that a parent who is loving, affectionate, consistent, and predictable, and who sets reasonable boundaries to reward good behavior and discourage bad behavior, creates a "secure" attachment with their child. In contrast, a parent who unpredictably doles out love or hostility and interacts in a smothering or withdrawn manner will inadvertently teach their child to attach in an insecure way. Children who have acquired a template for insecure attachment will play out this dysfunctional pattern in their future relationships—and will likely be disappointed with their quality of life. But just like anything else, this template can be changed through self-awareness regarding what behaviors are dysfunctional and how to correct them.

If we were told that we are worthy and capable, we grow up believing that, and even considering setbacks, we still value ourselves. But if we were told that we are worthless, unintelligent, hopeless, and incapable, we grow up believing that too, and setbacks further validate those lies. If you are a parent, you should cherish the incredible influence you have over your child's life beyond their years living under your roof. You create their life templates.

Our comfort zone becomes the relationship patterns that we know best—even if they are bad for us. When we lack awareness of our behaviors, we engage our subconscious mind. Unbeknownst to us, we may be trying to have a corrective emotional experience with our parent through our spouse as we project the past unresolved pain onto our current relationships; some may call this the generational curse. We see this play out in the movie *Encanto*, as Mirabel has the courage and strength to break the generational curse that was set into motion by Alma, her grandmother.

Repeating toxic patterns of relating is unhealthy for everyone involved. How do we stop it? *First,* we must become aware of our behavior and identify our patterns of interaction. *Second,* we must become curious about what thoughts and emotions set these behaviors into action. *Third,* is the underlying thought worth taking into our future? A thought that is true to your "I AM" and grounded in love will not result in destructive behaviors. *Fourth,* replace the old thought with a new one that is rooted in truth and love. *Fifth,* practice this thought by rehearsing it in your head and attaching a *fantastic feeling* to it—such as love, gratitude, joy, or peace. *Lastly,* visualize yourself putting into action your new thoughts and emotions. What sort of behaviors spring forth from this new mindset? *Believe it. Behave it. Become it.*

When changing your ways, be patient with yourself—after all, it took you years to form the negative subconscious programs that you are working diligently to deprogram and reprogram. Research states that it takes an average of 66 days for a behavior to become a habit. We will always have subconscious programs, but the goal is to ensure that they are rooted in love and truth—aka the *love program.* Your autopilot should result in interactions that produce peace and harmony. Let's not neglect the fact that when we improve our own behaviors, we must be patient with those around us, as they may be used to the dysfunction and chaos that we once produced. Give them time to get familiar with the new you.

Sometimes, we will revert to the old and dysfunctional programs during the process of reprogramming. This is *normal*. The dysfunctional programs have an established superhighway of neural networks that your new program is working to acquire. Over time, both cannot coexist. The more you practice the new program while engaging the cognitive control network (conscious awareness), the stronger it gets, weakening the dysfunctional program that is no longer being used. When you unintentionally fall back into the funk of the old program, get back up, dust yourself off, and reset. Do not use relapse as an excuse to not make positive change. In the next chapter, you will come to find that the choices you make now will impact your genetic output that will directly influence your offspring. There's no more room for dysfunctional programming—delete the programs! Upload the love program through your conscious awareness and get ready to embrace your divine design for your divine destiny. You were born to create!

Process Questions

➢ Identify the generational curses in your family.
➢ Are there any negative patterns of behavior that you have observed in your family that you do not wish to repeat?

    o What are they? Be specific.

➢ What faulty subconscious programs are you still operating on?
➢ What images come to mind when you think about your divine design?
➢ What do you imagine your divine design feels like?
➢ Do you think that you might be projecting unresolved emotional hurt on someone who did not cause the hurt?
➢ How did those who raised you interact with the world?

    o How did they manage stress?
    o How did they manage their emotions?
    o How did they see you?
    o Are your perceptions like theirs? How? Why?

➢ What good programs do you need to maintain?

Freedom Rhythm

➢ Please turn to page 180 to read about Freedom Rhythm and how to perform it.
➢ **Transformation Zone 3:**

    o **Visualization with bilateral stimulation:** *I want you to identify the changes you need to make to improve your family dynamic. Now, I want you to envision yourself putting those changes into action and you observing the positive effect on your family.*

- <u>Thought and emotion that inform your creative movement:</u>

  - <u>Dedicated Decision:</u> "I AM the miracle my family needs."
  - <u>Fantastic Feeling:</u> "Love."

- <u>Creative movement:</u> Now, put your experience into movement with your silk.
- <u>Positive Affirmation:</u> "I AM love! Yes, I AM!" x 3

Chapter 6

SUPERFICIAL LIFE RULES

"Everyone falls down. Getting back up is how you learn to walk."

WALT DISNEY

ONCE AGAIN, DISNEY BLEW MY MIND with their latest movie, *Elemental*. Among its many powerful underlying themes, the one that stood out to me, particularly as a psychologist, was a coming-of-age story wherein the protagonist must overcome *cognitive dissonance* to follow her heart. You read briefly about cognitive dissonance in chapter four but this time, we will explore how it affects our own *Hero's journey*. In short, *Elemental* is a movie about finding the courage to embrace our *true self*, despite what the world expects from us, and being loved for it.

Fire element Ember is an ambitious young woman determined to please her parents, Bernie (father) and Cinder (mother). Her parents left their home country to begin a new life in Element City, where they faced xenophobia (fear of the unknown) from other elements as they searched for a place to call home. Bernie and Cinder created a shop, The Fireplace, selling food and goods reminiscent of their home country and culture. Over the years, The Fireplace attracted many customers, becoming the central hub of the Fire District. Brought all the way from their home country located overseas, one of the key appeals of their store is the blue flame, a representation of the fire elements' heritage. Bernie's dream is to pass on his legacy to his daughter by giving her the shop upon his retirement. He is reluctant to retire, as Ember is not yet ready to manage the shop all on her own since she has tremendous difficulty controlling her temper, even as a fire element.

For as long as she can remember, Ember has convinced herself that the hard work of her parents must be repaid with her own hard work and sacrifice so that the legacy can endure. One day, Ember's father grants her the authority to independently run the store's red dot sale. The chaos of the customers triggers her to explode, which causes the store's pipes to burst, resulting in water damage and constant leakage. In the aftermath of the explosion, Ember meets Wade, a water element who accidentally gets sucked through the store's pipes during the explosion. Wade just so happens to be the city inspector, who begrudgingly writes Ember numerous citations related to the incident. Despite his incredible integrity which holds him accountable to the ticket writing, Wade has a huge heart and does everything in his power to help rectify the wrong related to the leaks and the impending doom of shutting down the shop because of its multiple water hazards. Ember keeps these interactions a secret from her parents because she does not want them to discover that her temper has led to the potential closing of The Fireplace.

In this process of trying to stop the closing of the shop and discovering the source of the leakage, Ember cultivates a beautiful friendship with Wade, who supports and encourages her to follow her heart. He gently urges her to explore the source of her explosive temper, and he hypothesizes that her spirit is trying to tell her something that she is not ready to hear. Ember dismisses his wisdom. Wow! I think that Wade has become my new favorite Disney character!

Wade opens Ember's eyes to … (sing with melody➔) "A whole new world, a new fantastic point of view, no one to tell us no, or where to go, or say we're only dreaming…" Seriously, they experience a very Aladdin and Princess Jasmine moment—but instead of a magic carpet, Ember creates a makeshift hot air balloon and powers it with her hotness.

An unexpected and never-before-seen romance blossoms between a princess and a pauper—correction—between fire and water elements. If you are catching the patterns repeated in Disney movies, you should certainly be catching your very own patterns of thinking, feeling, and behaving—how do you like that?!

Ember recognizes her talent for sculpting glass when she transforms sandbags into a tempered glass seal that serves as a dam to prevent the Fire District from flooding—one of the main factors contributing to the water leakage at The Fireplace. Ember's ingenuity absolves her tickets, and the store is temporarily saved. Ember meets Wade's family and impresses his mother by fixing a broken glass pitcher by sculpting it into a new and more fabulous design. Wade opens her eyes to the fact that Element City is made of glass skyscrapers and encourages her to cultivate and contribute her unique talent—her perfect self-expression, her divine design for her divine destiny! Wow, again! Is Wade a prince undercover?

Oddly, Ember's enlightenment leads her to confusion and deep sadness. She finally listens to Wade's advice and allows herself to listen to her spirit and in doing so, she realizes that she does not want to take over the family legacy. Ember learns that anger is not something to be overcome but rather something to be listened to as a guide. That same night, her father reveals his new and enlarged store sign that reads, "Ember's Fireplace" in bright neon lights. Ember stifles her emotions, and dutifully receives her new position upon his pending retirement. In doing so, she decides to abandon Wade, as her father would never approve of fire and water mixing.

Wade interrupts Bernie's retirement ceremony and professes his love for Ember and encourages her to speak her truth before it is too late. Ember dismisses Wade and during their lover's quarrel, it is revealed that Ember's temper was to blame for the damage caused by the burst pipes. Enraged by all that he has learned, Bernie revokes the store from Ember and renounces his retirement.

Hopeless and lost, Ember looks out at the glass skyline, contemplating her predicament, and while doing so, she notices that her glass dam has broken, and the flood is raging toward the Fire District. She rushes home to save her parents and to keep the blue flame burning. As she is surrounded by water, Wade comes to her rescue. The power of the flood pushes the blue flame, Ember, and Wade into a confined space. If they leave the space, Ember and the blue flame will be snuffed out by the flood; if they stay, Wade will evaporate from their heat. In his final moments, Wade professes his love for Ember and convinces her that he has no regrets because she inspired him and made his life worth living. Wade sacrifices his life for Ember and the blue flame as he quickly evaporates. After his perceived death, Ember has the courage to embrace her truth and share it with her family, who is grateful for Wade's immense love and immeasurable sacrifice. I seriously bawled during this scene, as I secretly wiped away my tears so my son wouldn't chastise me—and then I noticed that he was crying, too!

To everyone's surprise, Wade returns via emotional condensation—both a cathartic and comedic scene in the movie. Yes, Wade evaporated into the ceiling and returned as condensation when all was calm. In the end, Ember accepts her truth and follows her dream to become a glass sculptor, while Wade tags along for emotional support. Ember and Wade boldly continue their romance, as the mixing of their chemistry is magical. Ember's parents feel blessed that Ember survived the flood; consequently, they warmly receive Wade and support Ember as she blazes a new trail—just as they did many, many years ago. Bernie and Cinder enjoy the retired life after handing their shop over to their two most loyal customers. Bernie tells his daughter that the shop was never his dream. He continues to explain that the dream had always been Ember, and now that dream is fulfilled upon witnessing her fulfill her own dreams—her divine design for her divine destiny.

This is a summary of a beautiful story, and by no means does it do it justice or capture all the nuances. However, for the remainder of this chapter, this summary will help us to identify and highlight some very important psychological themes that we frequently encounter within our own lives. And yes, Prince Wade is officially my favorite Disney character—sorry Judy, maybe you'll redeem yourself in *Zootopia 2*!

The flow

MOST of the time
Thoughts→ Emotions→Behaviors

About 10 % of the time
Behaviors→Emotions→Thoughts

Extremely rare (true survival mode)
Emotions→Behaviors

Approximately ninety percent of our behaviors derive from our thoughts. In between our thoughts and behaviors are our emotions. Our emotional reaction to our thoughts serves as a catalyst that propels our behavior. What about that one percent of behaviors that do not arise from thought? Those behaviors arise from our survival response—the true emotional state of fear when our life is in danger. It is not the type of fear that emanates from our thoughts when we contemplate "worst-case scenario." It is the type of fear that relies solely on instinct and *skips thinking* because there is no time for it when faced with imminent threat. Moreover, there are circumstances wherein we intentionally change our behavior in hopes of shifting our mood to alter our thoughts. This is an intentional and strategic self-initiative that we do not always practice.

Thinking: If thoughts are the written words in a book, then our emotions are a magnifying glass that amplifies the written words (thoughts). If thoughts are the seed, then emotions are the flowers in bloom. If thoughts are the pebble thrown into the water, then emotions are the rippling waves. Your emotions are the magnetic part of your electromagnetic signature and can "amplify, bloom, ripple" or project ten feet from the center of your body via your aura. Don't forget, thoughts are the language of the mind and emotions are the language of the body. Together, thoughts and emotions create your electromagnetic signature (aura) and together, they set your behaviors into motion. Everything you do should fall in line with your thinking and your feeling, and how you think and feel should be grounded in truth and love.

Intermediate and core beliefs: Let's take it back to the subconscious mind that forms the programs we run today. Recall that from birth to the age of eight, we are downloading the programs of life from our primary caregivers. How they interacted with us, others, and the world at large became our internalized template, good or bad. It is during these years that we form the core beliefs that we will carry throughout our lives. Our intermediate beliefs and automatic thoughts arise from our core beliefs. Intermediate beliefs are the steppingstone between core beliefs and automatic thoughts. Intermediate beliefs interpret our experience through the lens of the core belief, using "if, then" rules. Automatic thoughts are like quick assumptions that follow the rules of our intermediate thoughts and consequently validate our core beliefs. These thoughts all result in an emotional experience that determines how we behave and what we manifest.

In the movie *Elemental*, Ember's core belief is "I am unworthy." Throughout the movie she expresses feeling unworthy of the great sacrifices her parents have made so that she could live an abundant life. Her intermediate belief is "If I repay their sacrifice with my own sacrifice, I will be worthy." An automatic thought is a quick reaction to a situation or circumstance. Ember has a difficult time managing challenging customers. To help her manage her temper, her father instructs her to "take a breath and make a connection." The first time we observe Ember lose her temper is when a pesky customer demands a free sparkler after reading the sign buy-one-get-one-free. He declares that he only wants the free one. Ember corrects him multiple times, explaining that you must buy one to get one free. The customer dismisses her correction and insists that the "customer is always right!" At this point Ember explodes and her father intervenes to placate the customer and excuse her behavior. Her automatic thought in response to this situation could be, *I will never get it right!*

Let's look at the emotions and behaviors that spawn from Ember's core belief of "I am unworthy." Ember may feel sad, angry, frustrated, confused, disappointed, and even emotionally exhausted. With the objective to improve her mood and to prove herself worthy to her father, Ember overcompensates for her mistakes. We see this when she volunteers to take on more responsibilities within the shop and competes with her father's delivery time. Her behaviors reflect her desire to be worthy in the eyes of her family. Our behaviors reflect our emotional state.

Fear as a driving force: Ironically, our negative core beliefs become our psychological fears. Yes, you are one step ahead! This is when the fear program takes over and dictates our decision-making process. We aim to succeed to avoid fear of failure. We aim to be worthy to avoid fear of unworthiness. We aim to please to avoid our fear of rejection. We aim to be stoic and composed to avoid our fear of vulnerability, and the list goes on. Being driven by fear of failure can result in success, though it is not truly fulfilling, because where there is fear, there is an absence of love and acceptance.

If our focus is on avoiding fear, fear then becomes our focus! Therefore, we must take caution because we attract what our thoughts and emotions are focused upon. We certainly do not wish to attract situations or scenarios that we inherently fear. Ember fears confrontation because it has the potential to evoke her temper, which disappoints her parents and reinforces her core belief and her fear of being unworthy. For as long as Ember continues to focus on this fear, she will attract confrontational situations that perpetuate the cycle. We observe this occurrence throughout the movie. The law of non-resistance is also in effect here. What Ember resists, persists!

Love as a driving force: When we lead with love, there is no fear. This means fully embracing your "I AM" and the thoughts that go with it! "I AM" successful. "I AM" worthy. "I AM" courageous enough to be vulnerable. "I AM" enough. You are who and what you believe you are. Ember unintentionally shows Wade all sides of her—the good, the bad, and the ugly. It is his unconditional love and acceptance that sets her free from the fear of not being enough. Wade sees Ember's superconscious mind—her divine design for her divine destiny! Eventually, Ember begins to see herself through his eyes. When Ember liberates her fear of disappointing others and accepts her truth, including her love for Wade as water element, her desire to explore the world, and her passion for glass sculpting, she sheds her "I'm" and steps into her "I AM"—her spiritual self grounded in truth and love. Upon doing so, her life is *no longer forced*, as she now *flows* with the spirit of harmony. When you discover your truth, the universe finds a way to open the doors to your destiny!

Allowing the thoughts of your "I AM" to take precedence means that positive emotions and behaviors will follow. Your "I AM" is the most powerful electromagnetic signature to connect with the universe to manifest your dreams. It operates on a limitless mindset that possesses a *dedicated decision* of the dream and a *fantastic feeling* of *gratitude* for the dream coming true. This cognitive and emotional mindset prepares the body to receive the miracle and motivates it to act in line with your dream fulfilled, and so it will be!

Feeling: Emotions are the action catalyst—an energetic wave that flows from our thoughts to our behaviors. Emotions exist to compel the body to act (behaviors) for the purpose of fulfilling the desires of the mind (thoughts). In Latin the derivative for the word emotion is *emotere*, which directly translates to *energy in motion.*

Let's talk neuroscience. Emotions are chemical reactions to past experiences. As our senses record incoming information from the environment, clusters of neurons organize themselves into networks. When they freeze into a particular pattern, the brain makes a chemical that is sent throughout the body. How this energetic experience is physically felt is an emotion. Recall that thoughts are the language of the mind, while emotions are the language of the body. The stronger the emotional quotient from an event—good or bad—the stronger the change in our internal chemistry. The stronger the change in our internal chemistry, the more vivid the memory. We remember events better when we remember how the event made us feel.

Positive emotions energetically spiral upward and outward, expanding to those nearby. This lively energy brightens our electromagnetic signature (aura) that communicates with the universe and is contagious to those who are receptive to it. Positive emotions trigger muscle expansion and relaxation, producing brain and heart coherence. In contrast, negative emotions spiral downward and inward, narrowing into our body like a laser. They cause muscle tension and muscle contraction. Most people dismiss this energy because it is too emotionally distressing to deal with it. This results in a buildup of toxic energy within our body that negatively affects every single cell.

Suppressing our negative emotions results in psychological, spiritual, and physical congestion that is terrible for our health.

Emotional energy in and of itself is neutral. Our psychological and physical reactions, what we think and how we physically feel, determine whether the emotional energy becomes positive or negative. Think of emotion as a pulsating wave that transports our spectrum of feelings. It is fluid energy that is meant to be acknowledged, felt, released, or transformed. Positive emotion should be shared, while negative emotion should be transformed into positive productive energy or simply expelled. We thrive when we learn how to transform emotion, whether positive or negative, into productive action that promotes feelings of peace and joy for ourselves and others. Understanding this improves our emotional intelligence.

Emotional congestion: Just as a volcano erupts because of density and pressure, we are prone to erupt from the buildup of negative energy. A negative emotional reaction over time becomes a mood. If this emotional energy is not intentionally liberated, released, transformed, or set free, it becomes a temperament. The longer this negative emotional state endures, the more hard-wired it becomes in our brain, creating its very own set of neural network superhighways that are programmed with congruent thoughts and behaviors. It creates its own outlook and what was once a temperament becomes an enduring personality. A personality grounded in a negative emotional state is toxic to the body and everybody. It's imperative for you to release negative emotional energy as soon as you or someone else detects it. We must embrace self-introspection to avoid the downward spiral that knocks the life right out of us. We need to ask ourselves if this is an emotion that we want to take into our future. It is imperative that we shorten our negative emotional refractory periods by transforming or liberating negative emotional energy to preserve our spiritual and physical health, as well as the quality of our relationships.

ElectroMAGNETIC signature: Emotions are the most important part of our electromagnetic signature that connects with the universe via the quantum realm. If emotions are the energetic wave connecting our thoughts to our 3D experience, we need to learn how to harness this incredible power. This means that we must emotionally teach the body what our desired future is going to feel like. That is why we identify a *dedicated decision*—the change we need to make to manifest our dreams—along with a *fantastic feeling*—how we feel upon receiving the manifestation. The go-to emotion that confirms receipt of the desired dream is gratitude. The more we energize this emotion, the more we will experience things to be grateful for. If you want to have a limitless life, you better start by feeling limitless!

Emotions in the body: Recall that our emotions are the language of our body. Let's take a moment to listen to what our body is trying to convey. Allowing yourself to authentically experience your emotions without rationalizing them is the first step to emotional freedom. At first, decoding your body's messages may seem tricky. The only wrong way to do it is to be judgmental toward your experience. Instead, start with childlike curiosity as you simply notice the physical sensations of your body. When you get out of your head, your body will provide insight and guidance.

In this process allow yourself to experience the feeling you didn't have the opportunity to release at the time of the event. Your body may be internalizing negative energy in motion that can manifest as heavy, tense, cold, shivering, or tingling sensations. In contrast, positive energy in motion may elicit physical sensations of lightness, warmth, softness, expansion, and flooding. We tend to want to expand and share positive emotion and expel or transform negative emotion. Visualization, deep breathing, and movement are ways to move emotion. Naturally, Freedom Rhythm focuses on releasing emotion through movement. After releasing your emotions, you can return to your analytical mind and align your emotional relief with healthy thoughts that encourage self-love, forgiveness, compassion, and hope. As with any new behavior, regular practice will make listening to your body easier as you discover your unique emotional patterns.

Behaving: Our behaviors reflect our emotional state. When we are happy, we want to do more. When we are sad, we lack the desire to do much of anything. In the world of psychology, we use the term *behavioral activation*. In fact, psychologists encourage their patients to increase their behavioral activation during depressive episodes. Research has proven that being active and doing things that produce a sense of accomplishment improves our mood.

Groundhog Day: Our thoughts and feelings influence the choices (behaviors) we make each day. These choices result in the experiences we create for ourselves. When we are stuck on autopilot, we select predictable experiences—maintaining a routine—eliminating the opportunity to experience something new and filled with possibility. Essentially, we are living the past on repeat, much like the old movie *Groundhog Day* featuring Billy Murry. This is when our today is a repeat of yesterday. The thinking, feeling and behaving loop constantly reinforces itself, creating a neural network superhighway for all our routines. It is challenging to gather sufficient energy to break free of the old energetic bonds associated with our routines. Changing our behaviors is one of the most effective monkey wrenches we can throw into the system to stop the autopilot that has consumed our life. It's time for new thoughts and new emotions! How can you create when you are stuck?

Backward strategy: Once we have identified that our negative thoughts are keeping us stuck, we can alter these thoughts by partaking in a behavior that is incongruent with them. We are capable of intentionally changing our behavior to improve our mood, which then results in transformed thinking. This is an intentional and strategic self-initiative. For example, Ember wholeheartedly believed that dating and romantic love was a waste of time—especially between two different elements! Moreover, when Wade asked her on a date, she made excuses consistent with her thoughts on romance. Breaking her routine to try something new seemed absurd to Ember, who worked tirelessly to gain the approval of her parents. She did not have time for fun and hence did not know how to have fun. Dating was so far out of her comfort zone that she rationalized every excuse not to partake. In fact, she told Wade not to count on her showing up. Ember ended up mustering the strength to break the energetic bond between herself and her routine to try something new. Going on a date was a behavior that was incongruent with her thinking. Ember enjoyed her time exploring the city with Wade and in doing so her mood improved and her thoughts on dating shifted, so much so that she agreed to more dates, which eventually blossomed into true love and a new and improved outlook on romance.

Another way that behavior is used to precipitate change in our thinking and feeling is through exposure therapy. This is when we intentionally expose ourselves to non-threatening situations that we fear, such as public speaking, with the intent of reducing the fear over time. The process of overcoming the fear is called *desensitization*, and the psychological technique used is exposure therapy. Many combat veterans fear being in crowds because of their frequent exposure to suicide bombers while on deployment. This fear is not conducive when they return from deployment and want to improve the quality of their family life by enjoying public outings like Disney World. A therapist may instruct her patient, a combat veteran, to go to Walmart during peak hours and stay there until their heartrate drops and their fear subsides. Over time, changing our behavior for the purpose of reprograming our thoughts and emotions can significantly improve our quality of life.

Just Breathe: Here is a one-size-fits-all behavior that is beneficial for all of us. Believe it or not, breathing is considered a behavior. When we learn how to control our breathing, we can change our mood, slow down our thinking, and alter the content of our thoughts. This is another way to use our behaviors as a source of psychological change.

Most people only think about the power of deep breathing to help calm and soothe their anxious and worried minds. We often leave out the benefit of breathing quickly to help energize us. To improve our focus and concentration we can practice the breath of fire, a yoga-informed technique wherein you breathe quickly, like a panting dog. The inhale is passive, and the exhale is powerful. This can take us from a sleepy state to an awakened state faster than a cup of coffee!

In contrast, when we are stressed, scared, nervous, anxious, or worried, we breathe fast and shallow. This quick breathing is triggered by our sympathetic nervous system, which activates our survival response. The quick breath is an attempt to oxygenate the blood and hasten its flow throughout our body to spread the neurochemical cocktail of chaos (adrenaline, cortisol, endorphins, etc.). To counteract this response—when your life is not imminently at risk—breathe slowly and deeply to trigger the vagus nerve, which is responsible for activating the parasympathetic nervous system that works to calm us.

Here are some benefits of deep breathing: It reduces stress hormones circulating in the body; it improves sleep, immunity, posture, and blood flow; it serves as a natural painkiller; and it reduces inflammation. I recommend engaging in deep breathing multiple times a day to receive the benefits listed above, as such practice enhances its effectiveness during times of high stress. Coupling deep breathing with positive visualization can be even more powerful. *Box breathing* is a useful deep breathing technique to reduce our anxiety and to regain our focus on the task at hand. It is used by Navy Seals while in combat: Inhale slowly by filling your lungs with air for a total of four seconds; hold your breath for four seconds; exhale slowly by releasing the air in your lungs for four seconds; and finally hold your breath for four seconds prior to repeating the process and beginning again with inhalation.

Changing our behaviors is a practical tool to neurohack negative thinking and feeling traps. Get creative with how you choose to make changes in your life.

Artificial life rules and cognitive dissonance

Living a life that is not in line with your true self ("I AM") results in *cognitive dissonance*. It occurs when we have conflicting thoughts, particularly when our "I AM" clashes with our "I'm." Recall that it is our goal to flow and not force, as flow comes from a place of trust and love, while force comes from a place of fear. Our thoughts, emotions, and behaviors should flow naturally and in alignment. Ideally, we flow from our "I AM," our spiritual identity, which means that our thoughts are in line with love and truth. These thoughts include "I AM" whole, strong, courageous, beautiful, intelligent, worthy, lovable, peaceful, kind, generous, grateful, fun, compassionate, brilliant, creative, etc. Flowing from these thoughts produces positive emotions and behaviors that are harmonious.

Recall that the "I'm" is our identity as defined by the world. Sometimes our culture and traditions passed on from one generation to the next dictate how we should think, feel, and act. It may even be the culture that you are caught up in on your social media. It is everything that we *allow* to influence our life as a set of hard or soft rules to abide by for the purpose placating the people around us or simply "belonging." Let's refer to these perceived cultural mandates as *artificial life rules.* To satisfy these *artificial life rules,* we may compromise our "I AM." Too often we stay stuck living a life that is not true to our "I AM" for fear of disappointing others. This is *cognitive dissonance,* and with it comes anxiety! Sometimes the fear of disappointment is so great that we snuff out our "I AM" as much as possible, which can lead to terrible health problems that we will address in the next chapter.

Wade was right when he told Ember that her anger outbursts were because her spiritual self was trying to communicate an important message to her—if she would only listen. Ember's anger was her reaction to her "I AM" trying to break free. The more time Ember spent with Wade, the more she was exposed to a new and enchanting world that fascinated her. Wade could see Ember's spirit—her true "I AM"—the reason he fell in love with her. He was relentless in his pursuit of her acknowledging her truth. Ember came to recognize that her "I AM" clashed with her *artificial life rules.* She had a life-altering decision to make: 1.) Choose to squash her "I AM" and embrace her artificial life rules to please her parents. 2.) Choose to let go of her *artificial life rules* to fully embrace the path of her "I AM" and potentially disappoint her parents.

It took a near-death experience for her to have the courage to embrace her truth and choose the path of her "I AM." As scary as it was, the *spirit of harmony* helped everything come together—even the love and acceptance of her parents. In the end, Ember's parents fanned her flame so that she could shine brighter—and not just because she was a fire element. Even though Ember chose to embark upon her own spiritual journey, she could still pay homage and respect to her parent's culture, partaking in events that didn't cause her to experience any *spiritual friction.* We can still honor and respect the *artificial rules of life* without having to internalize them.

We have watched every Disney protagonist—Ember, Moana, Elsa, Remy, Wreck-It-Ralph, Vanellope Von Schweetz, Arial, Aladdin,

Jasmine, Rapunzel, Simba, Nala, Belle and the Beast, Judy, Nick, etc.—release their *artificial life rules* to step into their "I AM." It is the most critical part of the Hero's journey. Choosing your "I AM," no matter what the cost, can be terrifying—though it is the only way to finally be set free. Those who love you will not leave you. It may take time for them to emotionally process everything, but in the end, they will admire your strength. Who knows, they may even wish to be set free, too! You are not alone in how you feel. Every time you do something courageous, you inspire someone else to do the same. If you want to create, you must first be set free!

Process Questions

- ➤ What "if-then" thinking rules have you created for yourself?
- ➤ Identify your positive and negative automatic thoughts.
- ➤ Identify the underlying core beliefs of your negative automatic thoughts.
- ➤ Are you experiencing cognitive dissonance? About what?
- ➤ Can you identify a "Wade" in your life—someone who is a safe emotional space?

  - o Who are you a "Wade" to?

- ➤ What artificial life rules can you identify in your life?
- ➤ What can you do to change up your routines?
- ➤ What behaviors can you use to neurohack your life on "rerun?"

Freedom Rhythm

- ➤ Please turn to page 180 to read about Freedom Rhythm and how to perform it.
- ➤ **Transformation Zone 3:**

  - o **Visualization with bilateral stimulation:** *I want you to quiet your body and mind to listen to your spirit. What is your spirit trying to convey to you? What does your spirit need you to do so that you can live out your divine design?*
  - o The mindset that informs your creative movement:

    - ▪ Dedicated Decision: "I AM spiritual."
    - ▪ Fantastic Feeling: "Peace."

  - o Creative movement: Now, put your experience into movement with your silk.
  - o Positive Affirmation: "I AM spiritual! Yes, I AM!" x 3

Chapter 7

ENERGETIC TRANSFERENCE

"Life is composed of lights and shadows, and we would be untruthful, insincere, saccharine if we tried to pretend there were no shadows."

WALT DISNEY

MOANA MAY VERY WELL BE the most courageous and selfless of all the Disney protagonists, as she follows the guidance of her spirit to fix the wrongs of others for the purpose of rescuing her people. Her spirit is her "I AM," her highest self that is formed in truth and love, connecting directly with the universe. Many people use the term soul and spirit interchangeably, as if they were the same, but that is not the case.

Our soul is the essence of our being—it is who we are. One might say that our soul is our mind or free will. It is responsible for our thoughts, emotions, and behaviors. In the last chapter, we discussed that the ideal *flow of existence* begins with thoughts formed in love and truth that spring forth from our superconscious mind—our "I AM." Thereafter, high frequency emotions and positive behaviors flow from this abundant thought life. Similarly, there exists a spiritual order that flows harmoniously when our body surrenders to our soul that surrenders to our spirit ("I AM").

We encounter difficulty tuning into the frequency of our spirit when our soul and our body are creating energetic interference. When our soul rages with negative thoughts and emotions like confusion, frustration, anger, doubt, and even poor self-esteem, we cannot hear our spirit over all this energetic noise. Moreover, our body chimes into this energetic interference when it experiences any sort of lack—lack of sleep, lack of health (pain), or lack of satiation (hunger and cravings of all sorts). It is when we can learn to quiet the energetic cacophony of our body and soul that we can connect to the frequency of our spirit. When our lives are chaotic and disharmonious, there is often chaos and disharmony brewing within us.

To fulfill her mission Moana had to tune into the frequency of her spirit. In doing so, she had to quiet the doubt in her mind that was reinforced by her parents' disapproval of her desire to sail across the ocean. She also had to quiet her body that endured the pain of multiple sailing wrecks, as well as sleepless nights spent navigating her voyage. Also, we never see her eat! When I'm hangry (hungry and angry because of it) there is no spiritual frequency loud enough to keep me in line. Feed me first! Last, there are negative consequences for the mind and body when the frequency of our spirit cannot be accessed. Let's explore Moana's voyage and see if you can point out the laws of karma, forgiveness, grace, and freedom in action.

Te Fiti is the beautiful goddess of nature who brought to life the ocean and many Polynesian islands, including Motunui. Her power to create originates from her heart, a pounamu stone that's lodged deep in the lush mountainside. Maui the trickster, shape-shifting demigod of the wind and sea, as well as the master of wayfinding, stole the heart from Te Fiti as she rested. He did this with the intention of giving the heart to mankind so that they may possess the power of creation. Upon losing her heart, Te Fiti, the embodiment of nature, began to crumble, spreading death and disease throughout the islands and chaos within the ocean. Upon stealing the heart, Maui encountered Te Ka, a volcanic demon, who battled him for possession of it. Two things were lost to the depths of the ocean that day, Te Fiti's heart and Maui's magical fishhook that granted him the power to shapeshift.

A thousand years later, the ocean lures a small toddler into its shallow waters and reveals the glowing heart of Te Fiti. Drawn to the luminescence of the heart, the toddler takes it into her possession, only to drop it on the shore when her father scolds her for wandering too close to the tides. Sixteen years later that toddler has grown into a young woman who is next in line to become chief of the island of Motunui. Her name is Moana and she is eager to become a wise, strong, and compassionate chief. The death and disease caused from the loss of Te Fiti's heart has spread to the island of Motunui, destroying their vegetation and making fishing impossible in the tumultuous ocean. Frustrated with the dire circumstances of her people, Moana looks to her grandmother, Tala, for spiritual guidance.

Eager to help guide Moana on her spiritual journey, Tala brings her to a sealed-off cavern. There, Moana discovers ancient sailboats and learns that her ancestors were once voyagers who spent most of their days navigating the oceans. Voyaging was the spiritual calling of her people, and now fear of the turbulent waters keeps them from it. Tala tells her the story of Te Fiti's stolen heart and that it is the reason for their island's decay and the ocean's discord. She also reveals to Moana that the ocean gave her the heart when she was small. Tala explained that she kept it safe for Moana until she came of age. That same night, Tala falls ill and in her final moments instructs Moana to find Maui and make him restore the heart to Te Fiti.

Moana urgently packs her belongings, selects her sailboat, and takes off into the darkness of the ocean. To light her path, the spirit of Tala takes the form of a giant stingray and guides her past the reef to Maui's destination. Moana weathers a terrible storm that night and serendipitously wrecks on the island on which Maui is stranded. Maui attempts to imprison Moana and steal her sailboat but he fails. Begrudgingly, the two venture off to retrieve his magical shape shifting fishhook from Tamatoa, a giant coconut crab.

As much as we want to despise Maui for all the trouble he has caused, in addition to his narcissistic personality, we come to learn his truth through Moana's gentle coaxing. As an infant he was discarded into the ocean by his parents. The Gods took pity on him, saved him from drowning, and bestowed him with the title of demigod, gifting him with his magical fishhook. Maui's deep hurt from his parents' abandonment has played out in his desire to receive approval from humanity. To prove that he was worthy of love, he bestowed many gifts upon them, including the heart of Te Fiti. Maui's intention was to give humanity the power to create, and in doing so, he would finally prove himself worthy of love.

Maui and Moana come to respect one another just before their first encounter with Te Ka the volcanic demon. Te Ka guards the island where Te Fiti rests. In an intense battle, Te Ka overpowers Maui and severely damages his fishhook, impeding his ability to shapeshift. Frustrated and angry with the outcome of the battle, Maui gives up the fight and abandons Moana, who loses all hope. In her hopelessness, Moana has a supernatural encounter with her grandmother and her ancestors. They remind her of her strength and let her know that she has made them proud and that they love her no matter what she chooses.

Determined and encouraged, Moana decides to restore the heart herself. As she approaches the island of Te Fiti, Te Ka attacks her relentlessly, and to her surprise, Maui returns and intercepts the blows until his fishhook is completely obliterated. This gives Moana the opportunity to reach the island where Te Fiti rests. Moana is confused when she discovers that where Te Fiti once rested, there is now an empty hole in the earth—Te Fiti is gone.

In the final scene, Moana shows Te Ka the heart. The ocean obeys Moana's request to part itself so that Te Ka can reach her. Moana walks confidently toward Te Ka and everything happens in dramatic slow motion. In rage and fury Te Ka storms across the ocean bed like a giant compared to the size of Moana. With love and compassion, Moana sings to Te Ka, "I have crossed the horizon to find you. I know your name. They have stolen the heart from inside you, but this does not define you. This is not who you are. You know who you are—who you truly are!" Moana places the heart into Te Ka's chest and instantaneously Te Ka transforms back into Te Fiti the Goddess of Nature.

The return of Te Fiti's heart heals the islands and the ocean. Maui apologizes to Te Fiti and she restores his fishhook and Moana's sailboat. Victorious, Moana gleefully returns to her island and becomes their beloved chief and wayfinder. Maui joins her and finds a place where he authentically belongs. This is a story about the cycle of spiritual hurt, its consequences, and its deep and profound healing.

Transferring energetic hurt

Everything is energy in motion. The more we operate on the *fear program,* consumed by chaos, need for control and predictability, anxiety, chronic stress, and an underlying theme that sounds something like "I'm not enough," the more forced our energetic flow becomes. Recall that when fear is our *driving force,* our electromagnetic signature dims, resembling that of an inanimate object. You may even feel it when you move—tight, dense, and drained in the absence of energy. When your *driving flow* comes from the *love program,* you are more energy than you are matter. You can even feel it when you move, as there is a lightness in your step.

Love is pure and the original source of energy that connects us all. We are the ones who have injured and scarred this energy because of our fears and selfish desires. Energetic pain and suffering have twisted, manipulated, contorted, contaminated, and damaged what was once love. Our energetic hurt becomes too much to bear on our own so we displace it to those around us—intentional or not. The displacement of energetic hurt creates a ripple effect—just like a stone tossed into a placid lake that ripples outward and stops only until the energy has been depleted. We have a choice to be conduits of this hurtful energy and continue to pass it on, or to recognize it, stop it, and liberate it.

How do we liberate energetic hurt when it hits us? First, we identify that this energy is the product of someone who is hurting. If the hurtful energy is transferred to us by someone we wish to help, we show compassion for the energetic hurt and we return it with love, which has the power to disarm it. If it is someone we don't know, we transform the energy into something beautiful and productive, grounded in truth and love, or we simply release it. We may choose to release the energy through movement (exercise) or meditation (prayer). It is absolutely our responsibility to stop the transfer of negative energy when it hits us. If we stop it, we eliminate unnecessary hurt and suffering, and by doing so, we raise the collective conscience of the entire world. Many have lost their "I AM" due to receiving energetic hurt during a vulnerable time.

Maui's energetic hurt caused by his parents' rejection of him at birth and their attempt to drown him in the ocean deeply wounded his soul. Maui could've transferred that energy into wreaking havoc upon humankind but instead he used that energy to gain their love and approval. Stealing Te Fiti's heart was a sacrifice he made to earn love because he felt unworthy of it. This gesture came from a place of fear, as Maui felt he was not enough. His heroic gestures to humankind were his attempts to purchase love—but love is not for sale. Moreover, his haughtiness and narcissistic personality were defense mechanisms used to cope with feeling unlovable. Maui stole Te Fiti's heart to fill his heart, leaving her with an even greater void. Te Fiti's hurt contaminated the world and transformed her into the volcanic demon Te Ka. When we feud with one another, we are on different energetic frequencies. The energetic frequency of love is the common ground wherein all parties can find peace and harmony—but someone must be brave enough to lead the way by being the first to surrender their sword. In the end, both Maui and Te Fiti end up losing, until Maui musters the courage to acknowledge his wrongs, as he works to restore both of their hearts. This is both the law of forgiveness and freedom in action. When Maui embraces the truth, he is set free, Te Fiti is set free, and all of nature is set free. Do you see how the healing of one person can result in the healing of many?

Maui demonstrated his strength through his *vulnerability* when conveying his truth to Moana. Her spiritual wholeness, accompanied by her love and acceptance of Maui's pain, was the energetic catalyst that set his healing into motion. In the presence of Moana, Maui felt as though he were enough. Psychologists label this demonstration of love, acceptance, and empathy for another person as <u>unconditional positive regard</u>. In fact, Carl Rogers created *Person-centered therapy,* which diverged from the traditional models of therapy wherein the therapist took on a more distant role as the "expert." Instead, his objective was for the therapist to meet the patient where they were at in their hurting and compassionately provide unconditional positive regard—the primary treatment modality.

Moana had the courage to follow her spirit, and in doing so, she was able to discover her incredible talents—gifts she would have never uncovered otherwise. Moana brought the energies of Maui and Te Ka together and flooded them with love to the point that they could not deny it—until all they could do was receive it, and then become it. Moana was born to create peace and love, along with every good thing that springs forth from it. When truth and love lead the way, energetic growth and healing manifests, and the law of harmony kicks into action to right all the wrongs.

Energetic vessels

In our simplest form, you and I are vessels. The purpose of a vessel is to be poured into and to pour out of. The word pouring connotes the flow of energy which is emotion. For most of our experiences, we choose what we allow into our lives and our minds, but there are unfortunate times wherein we have no control over what confronts us. During these times we may feel congested with negative energy (emotions) caused by a disheartening experience that shook our spirit. According to the *law of conservation of energy*, energy cannot be created nor destroyed, only transferred or transformed from one form of energy to another. If we do not transform or expel this negative energy that dims our electromagnetic signature and causes energetic spiritual hurt, our vessel becomes congested and eventually damaged. The hallmark symptom of post-traumatic stress is avoidance, meaning we don't want to deal with the hurt, so we ignore it. When we avoid dealing with this toxic and negative energy our vessel (body) becomes congested and contaminated, almost like being poisoned from the inside out. We must find a way to release this putrid energy before it makes us sick. Even the characters in Moana experienced negative physical effects from internalizing negative energy. Maui lost his ability to shapeshift, and Te Fiti turned into Te Ka the lava demon, whose negative energy polluted all of nature. If it happens in a Disney movie, it must be true! All joking aside, let's dive deeper into this phenomenon and learn about the study epigenetics, so that we may never experience these horrific side effects.

You are not a victim to your genetics

Genes are blueprints to the basic building blocks of life—proteins. I want you to imagine your body like a blueprint to a home. This blueprint has an established floor plan and square footage—just like your genetic code—but you decide everything else. First, what foundation will you build your home on? *Therefore, everyone who hears these words of mine and puts them into practice is like a wise man who built his house on the rock. The rain came down, the streams rose, and the winds blew and beat against that house; yet it did not fall, because it had its foundation on the rock (Matthew 7:24-25).* Will you choose a reputable builder? Are you invested in purchasing quality materials? What style of flooring and cabinetry will you select? How about the back splashes and color schemes? Will your home be designed to entertain guests? Do you want your home to have good natural lighting? How many windows will you install? Do you see the point I'm trying to make? Your decisions or lifestyle choices often have greater influence than your genes alone. We can both agree that a thoughtfully constructed house will last longer than one that comes in a box and has questionable assembly instructions from that four-letter company.

Epigenetics is the study of how our environment impacts our genetic expression—essentially, the output of our genes. Let's break down the word epigenetics. In Latin, *epi* means "on top of" or "over." This poses the question—what is over our genes? The answer: *our mind.* It goes like this—mind over genes—which implies that our thoughts, emotions, and behaviors have a vote in our genetic output. You may be wondering if you can change your eye or hair color just by engaging in intense thought or visualization about this, but that is inaccurate. Physical characteristics, such as those mentioned, remain stagnant, as they are part of the blueprint. However, there are fluid genetic traits that can change, such as personality (angry, aggressive, peaceful, etc.), predisposition to disease (cancer, alcoholism, addiction, etc.), and overall health.

Our environment includes many variables, such as where we live, how we behave and interact with the world—healthy or not—and most importantly, our psychological mindset—positive or negative. There is scientific proof that we are not victims to our genes. In fact, our mindset has a major impact on our cellular function.

Recall that your mind tells your brain what neurochemicals to produce. The chemistry of love enhances cell growth and vitality because of the presence of oxytocin and endothelial derived relaxing factor within your bloodstream. This is the chemical environment that surrounds your cells. In contrast, the emotion of fear produces the neurochemical cocktail of chaos (cortisol, adrenaline, noradrenaline, endorphins, etc.) that flows through your bloodstream, also surrounding your cells. The chemical environment surrounding your cells can influence your genetic expression.

Back in the day, Biology 101 taught us that the most important part of a cell was its nucleus. Scientists are recanting this notion and emphasizing the importance of the cell membrane. Essentially, the cell membrane serves as the gatekeeper that determines what chemical signals from the surrounding environment flow in and out of the cell, all of which have the potential to either up-regulate or down-regulate the cell's genetic expression.

Identical twins possess identical genes—yet their physical traits can vary drastically once the consequences of their life choices have been set into motion. During childhood, identical twins who are raised in the same household will possess matching physical and psychological attributes. In this situation, nature (their genes) and nurture (their environment) are the same. However, when they become adults, they venture out on their own to make big decisions about careers, lifestyle, where to live, who to marry, etc. The most crucial decisions are related to how they will manage stress.

The twin who chooses the "fast-paced" corporate lifestyle, lives by the mantra "work hard; play hard" and copes by consuming drugs and alcohol, may die of a heart attack in his early fifties. The other twin may choose to become an educator, get married, have kids, establish a healthy work-life balance, engage in spiritual practice, and use exercise and meditation as his primary means of coping and live to be 85 years old.

We observe the same trends in clinical research laboratories, wherein mice were bred to be genetically predisposed to disease—but those that were fed healthier food and placed in a more "relaxed" environment lived longer and consequently did not pass the diseased genes on to their offspring. Take a moment to reflect on how this occurrence relates to the programs you choose to live by: fear or love. How you choose to wire your brain now impacts your body all the way down to your genes—which in turn influences the genetic predisposition of your offspring. Now that's powerful.

Transgenerational trauma occurs when we pass on of the psychological and physiological side-effects caused by a traumatic event to later generations. This does not mean that we pass on the specific memory of the trauma, but rather the psychological state we exhibit after the trauma. Such characteristics may include anxiety, hypervigilance, and a depressive outlook. The primary means of transmission is the uterine environment during pregnancy, causing epigenetic changes in the developing embryo. The genetic component is further reinforced when children model their parent's anxious and avoidant behaviors and their way of interacting with the world. We observed this in the Disney movie *Encanto* as two generations are affected by Alma's (the grandmother) traumatized disposition. Recall that Alma tragically witnesses the death of her husband during an armed conflict and lives her life in fear because of it. It is Mirabel who stops the generational curse by sharing her insights—all of which were grounded in love and truth.

Research demonstrates that as few as five percent of cases of cancer and cardiovascular disease can be directly linked to genetic inheritance. What does that tell us? We are not victims to our genes; rather, our mindset has significant influence on this outcome. Spiritual and psychological disharmony can create a perfect storm for death and disease. Even when confronted with horrifying medical news, we can potentially change the outcome if we radically change our psychological and spiritual mindset and adopt the behaviors that flow from it. It's time to jump ship from the *fear program* and jump aboard the *love program's* cruise liner.

All thoughts, positive or negative, emit energy that can strengthen or weaken our physical health. The proteins produced by toxic thoughts are different than the ones produced by positive thoughts. Think of it like this: Tonic (positive) thinking produces tonic chemicals, while toxic thinking produces toxic chemicals. There is freedom in knowing that we are not doomed to become victim to our genes—and that we truly have the power in every way to create a life that exceeds our wildest imagination.

Process Questions

> ➤ Who can you give your unconditional positive regard to?
> ➤ How do you think the person who hurt you was hurt?
> ➤ How do you think you may have hurt others because of your hurting?
> ➤ How can you liberate your hurt?
> ➤ What sorts of choices are you making that are hindering your health?
> ➤ What can you do to quiet your soul and body to better hear your spirit?
> ➤ What is the truth that you need to acknowledge to be set free?
> ➤ What sort of genetic adversities run in your family?
>
>> o What things can you do to alter this?
>>
>>> ▪ How can you change your thoughts, emotions, and behaviors?

Freedom Rhythm

> ➤ Please turn to page 180 to read about Freedom Rhythm and how to perform it.
> ➤ **Transformation Zone 3:**
>
>> o **Visualization with bilateral stimulation:** *I want you to identify the things you need to change to be healthy (physical/ psychological/spiritual). I want you to envision yourself making such changes successfully. Now, I want you to see the final product—you as completely healthy in all areas of your life!*

- o <u>The mindset that informs your creative movement:</u>

  - <u>Dedicated Decision:</u> "I AM healthy."
  - <u>Fantastic Feeling:</u> "Gratitude."

- o <u>Movement:</u> Now, put your experience into movement with your silk.
- o <u>Positive Affirmation:</u> "I AM healthy! Yes, I AM!" x 3

Chapter 8

NEUROPOWER

"The way to get started is to quit talking and begin doing."

WALT DISNEY

I'S TIME TO BECOME FAMILIAR with the basics of neuroplasticity before we learn how to perform brain surgery on ourselves. All right, not literal brain surgery, but a lot of neurohacking to deprogram and reprogram our brains to our powerful "I AM." We must first grasp the concept of neuroplasticity before we can learn how to adaptively rewire our brains after traumatic and painful life events. Who do you think is the most "hard-wired" of the Disney protagonists?

I'd put my money on Ralph from *Wreck-It Ralph*. After all, he is a character in a videogame that is literally coded in 0's and 1's. His behavior is predictable both on and off the screen, and his personality matches the angry and destructive role that he portrays as the villain— after all, he is a program! Is there any hope for him break free from it? Ralph loathes being the "bad guy" whose role is to wreck an apartment complex so that the hero, a contractor named Fix-It Felix, comes to the rescue with his magic hammer to restore all the damage. He is awarded a shiny medal for his efforts, while Ralph is kicked off the ledge of a tall building, only to faceplant into a pile of mud. Ralph longs to be loved and appreciated like Fix-It Felix, but the characters in his game, the Nicelanders, are programmed to view him as the "bad guy"—nothing more and nothing less.

"I'm bad, and that's good. I will never be good, and that's not bad. There's no one I'd rather be than me," says Ralph in his Bad-anon group.

Ralph has internalized the belief, *I'm not enough.* This means his thinking and feeling is anchored in low self-worth. This is the message that his electromagnetic signature relays to the universe which attracts his 3D reality—one that is grounded in lack and a negative self-perception. We see this manifestation come to fruition by how the "Nicelanders" reject him, failing to recognize his worth despite the game being named after him—*Wreck-It Ralph.* Clearly, Ralph is operating in the fear program. Seeking to be appreciated, Ralph exits his game via the power strip and searches for a medal of honor by entering other games through Game Central Station. Ralph believes that if he is awarded a medal, just like Fix-It Felix, he will prove his worthiness to himself and the not-nice Nicelanders. He looks to the external world to supply his satisfaction and self-esteem, failing to realize that worthiness comes from within, as it is a conscious choice to embrace your "I AM." In his pursuit to become a hero, Ralph must leave his game, rendering his game defunct and pending shutdown in his absence. This incites havoc and fear amongst the Nicelanders.

> "Well, this may come as a shock to you, but in my game, I'm the bad guy, and I live in the garbage." -Ralph

> "No, not cool! Unhygienic, and lonely, and boring ... and that crummy medal was going to change all that. I go home with that baby around my neck and I'll get a penthouse, pies, ice sculptures, fireworks! Ah, it's grown-up stuff, you wouldn't understand," explains Ralph in his exchange with Vanellope.

Through a series of twists and turns, the universe grants Ralph the opportunity to befriend a character who is facing similar struggles of rejection and unworthiness. Notice how Ralph's state of mind (electromagnetic signature) attracted a character who reflects his inner emotional turmoil. Drawn together by their hurt and hope for a better tomorrow, Ralph and Vanellope become best friends. Confronting danger and potential death, Ralph saves Vanellope from being permanently eliminated from her game because she is a "glitch." Ralph is transformed by the love of this friendship and learns that he is truly courageous and heroic in the face of adversity. Moreover, the Nicelanders come to appreciate his valuable role in their game during his absence. Ralph's courage to embark on the Hero's journey forced him to confront new experiences that required him to show up and show out like never before, ultimately rewiring his brain—or should I say code? Ralph no longer identifies himself by his role in the game. He learns that he can play the important role of "bad guy" in his game but that he can also spiritually identify himself as the good guy and the hero in his own story. In Ralph's words, "Turns out I don't need a medal to tell me I'm the good guy."

Six years later, there is a sequel, *Ralph Breaks the Internet*, wherein Vanellope becomes bored and restless in her predictable routine as the lead player in her game, Candy Crush. A series of unfortunate gaming catastrophes becomes the catalyst that propels her to embark on the Hero's journey. Vanellope's spirit calls her to a new and action-packed adventure. While supportively accompanying her on her journey, Ralph discovers that throughout the years, he has become codependent on Vanellope's friendship. At the height of the journey, a virus clones a multitude of Ralph's insecurities. This takes on the exaggerated form of a giant codependent Ralph comprised of little Ralphs who are trying to capture Vanellope to satiate their neediness and insecurity. Again, the universe finds a dramatic way to reflect Ralph's inner emotional state right back at him. Do you think that the universe made it loud and clear? Ralph learns that love is freedom and the genuine ability to be happy for our loved ones when they discover their heart's highest calling. Though Vanellope's new game, Slaughter Race, is a long journey to Game Central Station, their relationship is not lost. Ralph and Vanellope capitalize on the benefits of technology, as they stay in touch via a virtual online chatting platform that is transmitted through holographic images. Ralph comes to discover that he is the source of his own joy and that his friends are the icing on his cake. Ralph unintentionally partook in a journey of deep self-introspection, and in doing so, he deleted the fear program that dictated his life and instead downloaded the love program that reprogrammed his brain to his great "I AM." Let's look further into the process of neuroplasticity and how it works to rewire the programs within our brain.

When the environment fills your void

In both movies, Ralph looked to fill the void caused by feeling unworthy and unlovable. At first, he believed that receiving a medal of honor would make him feel worthy, and in the sequel, he believed that his friendship with Vanellope was what made him lovable. When we look to the environment to be the source of our joy and fulfillment we will never be satisfied, because everything in the material world will eventually run out. We may look to retail therapy to fill the void, or plastic surgery, a new car, a vacation, or even substances like alcohol and drugs. In fact, we may even build a *tolerance* to these things over time, which means we need more of them to get the same sense of satisfaction we once did. Intentionally looking to the world to fix you often results in addictive behaviors. This also includes our relationships, as many people become co-dependent upon another person to make them happy, instead of being the creator of their own happiness. In a co-dependent relationship, you depend on another person to be the source of your emotional regulation. Depending upon the world to be our source of fulfillment is like being a thermometer—the temperature of your environment dictates your internal temperature.

The only thing that truly satisfies is the divine spirit of love that is found deeply and profoundly within you! It is your "I AM," because you are what you believe. Maybe you need to start believing that you are worthy, instead of looking to your friend to convince you of it. Maybe you need to start believing that you are limitless, instead of looking toward a substance that poisons your body so that you can feel limitless for a limited time. When we become addicted to relationships, stress, and substances our body becomes master to our mind. News flash:

You cannot create to your fullest protentional for the purpose of your divine design for your divine destiny when your BODY is MASTER to your MIND. Creating begins when your mind is master to your body. Even Ralph had to dig deep to discover that he is the source of his own joy. This meant letting go of the medal and allowing his friend to be set free. In doing so, he comes to recognize that he is far more than a unidimensional character but is rather a multidimensional design, capable of creating his own reality from the inside out. Be like the thermostat: Know the temperature you want to be, set it, and watch your environment become it!

Mind vs. brain

It's time for a quick review. Your brain is like a ball of globular goop—a big wad of spaghetti. This non-glamorous looking organ hosts approximately 86 billion brain cells known as neurons, and each neuron can make up to one thousand connections to other neurons. These connections are called *neural networks*. It is helpful for me to think of such neurons as stars and their connections as constellations—just as constellations come together to form an image, neural networks come together to form thoughts, memories, emotions, and behaviors. The funny thing is that the number of neurons in our head is nearly equivalent to the number of stars in our galaxy. Each person's brain is like its own galaxy!

Your mind is you. It is responsible for being the decision maker—it's your free will. What you choose to give your attention is what will manifest in your brain and become your experience from the inside out. Every moment of every day you are filtering what you allow into your brain and consequently what you put out. Think of your brain as the computer being dictated by your mind that selects which programs to run.

Let me give you a fascinating example of how the brain is slow to process in comparison to the mind. There is a phenomenon known as phantom limb. This occurs when someone loses an arm or a leg and can still feel sensations in it, as if it were still attached—hence, the term "phantom." After the removal of the limb, people often experience phantom pain in the location of the lost appendage. They explain the feeling of this pain as if the limb were still intact and stuck in the painful last position it was in prior to the amputation. Phantom pain can be excruciating and intolerable.

The treatment for phantom pain is mirror therapy, wherein a full-body mirror is placed at the center of the person's body, reflecting the healthy limb. Essentially, the person looks into the mirror, which creates a *completed* body image—appearing as if the missing limb is intact. The person freely maneuvers the healthy limb, and it appears as if both limbs are moving fluidly and without pain. Now, the mind is fully aware that the limb is missing—but the wiring of the brain has not caught up to this fact. More specifically, the brain's homunculus, the picture of the body on the motor cortex, continues to have a region dedicated to the sensation of the missing limb. However, when the brain sees the limb in the reflection as whole, intact, and in "good condition" it rewires its pain setting. Essentially, the mind is tricking the brain into rewiring itself. This is the magic of neuroplasticity!

A much easier example is when we watch an intense movie, and we experience the emotions alongside the characters. Whether our heartrate increases, and we hold our breath because the scene is so intense and action packed, or we shed tears because of the drama, our mind ultimately knows it's a movie, but our brain does not. Our mind is instructing our brain to release certain chemicals for the purpose of being entertained. Yet our brain is responding as if it were real life, especially when it releases cortisol and adrenaline that causes our hearts to pound and our palms to sweat.

Imagination: In a simple and unbelievable experiment, Drs. Guang Yue and Kelly Cole demonstrated that imagining using your muscles can actually strengthen them. The study looked at two groups, one that performed physical exercise and one that imagined doing exercise. Both groups exercised a particular muscle, Monday through Friday, for four weeks. At the end of the study the subjects who had done physical exercise increased their muscular strength by 30 percent, as one might expect. Those who only imagined doing the exercise, for the same period, increased their muscle strength by 22 percent. How is this possible? Well, during these imaginary muscle contractions, the neurons responsible for programming movement in the motor cortex were activated and strengthened, resulting in increased strength when the muscles were contracted. This is also a perfect example of how the brain does not know the difference between a real and an imagined experience—yet the mind does. Alright, let's close our eyes and imagine having a six-pack!!!

Neuroplasticity

Let's address how the choices you make play out on the cellular level, as neurons connect to form neural networks that eventually become superhighways within your brain. After all, these connections are responsible for your reality.

Neurons are information messengers that use electrical impulses and chemical signals to relay messages across the brain that affect your whole body. Your mind is responsible for creating these brain connections, which is called neuroplasticity. When you break down the term neuroplasticity you get "neuro" and "plasticity." Neuro means brain and plasticity means flexibility. When you put it together you get "brain flexibility."

Up until the early 90s neuroscientists believed that the brain was "fixed," which means that once developed, it did not change—except for the eventual deterioration that comes with age. Think about the mirror therapy we just discussed—that is neuroplasticity at its finest. We have seen the brains of patients radically reorganize themselves after severe traumatic brain injury (TBI). Severe TBI often results in immediate physical disability that obstructs the ability to walk, balance, move arms or legs, etc. However, after the intentional reorganization of the brain's neural networks through various techniques, those patients regained their physical functioning as new neural connections were formed.

In our early childhood our brain is the most neuroplastic. Enhanced neuroplasticity helps us to download all the programs we will need to "get through" life, from interpersonal dynamics to language acquisition. To master a skill as an adult, we must perform it approximately 10,000 times to become proficient at it. However, children only need to perform the skill approximately 5,000 times to achieve the same results. Neuroplasticity is all about learning and memory.

Here is a picture of two connected neurons that will come together with hundreds or thousands of other neurons to create a neural network—an information superhighway. To witness such an event, you would need a 10,000x power microscope. Neurons communicate with one another via electrochemical impulses.

NEUROTRANSMITTER

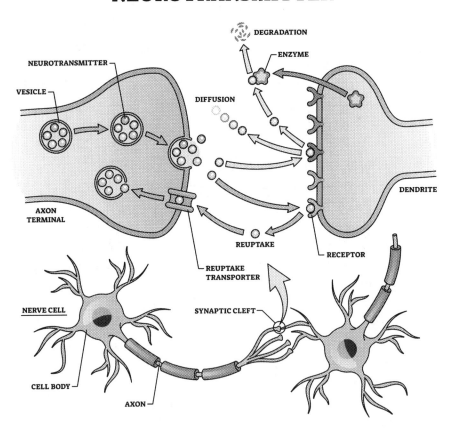

Every day you're choosing how to wire your brain—determining the neural networks that will form. These connections produce your thoughts, emotions, behaviors, ideas, memories, skills, and consequent life experiences. Obviously, you have created healthy and unhealthy neural networks. Our goal is to tear down those unhealthy networks and replace them with ones that are rooted in love and truth. Think of it like this...

Every time you learn something (riding bike, schoolwork, lecture, book, etc.), your brain forges a new neural network that physically changes the shape of it. When you recall what you have learned—like "jogging your memory"—your brain maintains and sustains these connections and they become stronger.

Neurons form relationships with other neurons, and the more they communicate with one another, the stronger their bonds (connections) become. It's like our human relationships: The more we interact with one another the "tighter" or stronger the relationship gets. When we stop interacting with one another, our relationships become distant, and our connections become weaker or non-existent. Neuroscientists say, "Neurons that fire together, wire together" and "use it or lose it."

Mountain trail

Let's use the mountain trail analogy to demonstrate how new thoughts and behaviors form neural networks. Your mission is to summit the mountain because you experience satisfaction at the top. You start at the base of the mountain at point A and you make your way to the summit at point B. No one has ever set foot on this mountain before—just as no one has ever thought your exact thoughts. Think of your brain as the mountain and your mind as the navigator that determines which trails to create.

This scenario focuses on how neural pathways are formed with a particular behavior, but this process is also applicable to the thoughts we choose to think. Imagine that you are a teenager who has observed your parents consume alcohol after a stressful day at work. You are left unsupervised after a bad day at school, and you decide to emulate your parents' drinking behavior to experience relief. You take your first sip of liquor, and it tastes awful. This first sip is like the first step in creating a trail up the mountain for the first time. You must use a machete to hack away all the wilderness that impedes your path. Each sip of alcohol gets easier and easier to consume. Finally, you summit the top of the mountain—you feel good—you feel buzzed—and your problems temporarily disappear until they come crashing down on you the next morning, amplified by a head-splitting hangover.

Drinking is addictive, and you have a genetic <u>pre</u>disposition to alcoholism because of your parents. Knowing all this, you make the choice to allow alcohol to alter your brain and your genetic code, as discussed in the epigenetics chapter. Now every time you have a bad day, you cope by hitting the bottle. Because your drinking behavior has become habitual, you have created a smooth and paved trail up the mountain. There is no longer a need to use your machete to clear the brush and forge the way. Fast forward into your adulthood, and that trail—actual neural network—becomes a superhighway to summit the mountain to "feel good." Now just the thought of alcohol triggers a release of happy molecules in your brain and instigates an intense craving. Clearly, alcoholism is unhealthy because of the negative effect it has on your body, your spirit, your relationships, your performance, your safety, and the overall danger it poses to your life in terms of drunken decision making. How do you stop drinking?

It starts by finding a new and adaptive means of coping with your stress, such as exercise, prayer, meditation, listening to music, running, yoga, journaling, etc. Let's say you choose to cope by taking long walks in your neighborhood while listening to your favorite jams. The first time you try this new method of coping after a stressful day, you will have to use your machete to create a new trail up the mountain to achieve relief. Fighting the alcohol craving is a challenge, but you must push through it long enough so that you can forge a new trail—a healthy one. The more you travel on the healthy trail, the smoother the trail gets, and the faster you reach the summit to experience relief.

The less you travel the "alcohol" trail, the more overgrowth occurs (like weeds and other vegetation) until finally it no longer exists, and that neural pathway becomes extinct, which is our ultimate objective. Both trails are competitive for your selection, as both trails cannot equally and effectively coexist at the same time. Relapse occurs when the old and maladaptive trail is chosen, as it may still be the dominant trail in the early stages of your healthy coping initiative. Sometimes relapse can be "reflexive and automatic." It is important to know that relapse is a part of recovery; however, we must make every effort to be accountable for our actions and immediately get back on track.

Sometimes certain people, places, things, or situations can trigger us while we are on our path to living a healthier and improved lifestyle. These triggers may temporarily take us back to old neural pathways that are unhealthy for us. For example, certain friends may bring back memories of an old way of life that may trigger cravings associated with it. Identifying your triggers is important, especially if you desire to neurohack old and disruptive neural pathways. It is helpful to avoid our triggers at the beginning stages of making change, until our new and adaptive neural pathways become strong superhighways capable of outperforming the old and maladaptive neural networks.

We must choose to form neural pathways that are grounded in the love program—everything that produces health and prosperity. These trails may be comprised of new ways of thinking that are rooted in our "I AM." Remember, the love and fear programs from which our thoughts and behaviors emanate cannot equally coexist at the same time. We must choose the program that we pour our energy into, and it will become the thriving program—our reality.

We possess a metaphorical "brain garden" and we choose what thoughts to prune, fertilize, and water. Similarly, we identify the bad thoughts, and like weeds, we pull them out by the roots so that they don't contaminate our garden, as they threaten to steal the life from our most precious vegetation. Each morning we wake up with a brand-new set of baby neurons, and we have the privilege *to choose* how to wire them.

Nowadays, we can access nearly everything instantaneously at the touch of a button. Gratification is not delayed like it once was. Our patience—well, that's like a muscle, and today's fast-paced rhythm doesn't require that we exercise it often. Our brain takes time to change. Research suggests that it takes three cycles of 21 days to change a behavior or a thought pattern. During that period, the new behavior or thought should be activated routinely.

You may have chosen to embark upon making radical and positive change by rewiring your brain (thoughts, emotions, and behaviors) to the love program, and I applaud your bravery in doing so. It is important to remember that your positive change is going to positively impact those around you; however, the people around you also need time to reprogram their brains to the new you. For example, Vanellope may become irritated with Ralph when he calls her, as she may expect him to act in the same old codependent and needy ways he once did. It will take time for her to reprogram her brain to the new Ralph, who is working diligently to be independent and supportive. Positive change requires patience for the brain to reprogram itself, patience for us to carry out the changes effectively, and patience for those who interact with us and who must adjust to our new and fabulous norm.

Neuroanatomy 101—The hand brain

> "My name's Ralph, and I'm a bad guy. Uh, let's see ... I'm nine feet tall, I weigh six hundred and forty-three pounds. Got a little bit of a temper on me. My passion bubbles very near the surface, I guess, not gonna lie." -Ralph

Place your hand with four fingers up and tuck your thumb into your palm. Your thumb and the bottom portion of your hand represent your midbrain, which is the emotion center, otherwise known as the limbic system. Within this system is the amygdala, the part of your brain that processes fear and threatening stimuli. As you know, when we operate from the midbrain, we are in survival mode and inclined to impulsive behaviors—we call this "flipping our lid." Throughout his movies, we've observed Ralph "flipping his lid" when he is angry and destructive—the sort of behavior that is reactionary and impulsive, which leads to poor decision making.

Now fold your fingers over your thumb to make a fist. This area of the brain represents your cerebral cortex, including the frontal lobe, which is the intelligent part of your brain. The frontal lobe is what makes you different than a chimpanzee, and it does not fully develop until the mid-twenties. You'll conveniently notice that this is the age when the cost of car insurance drops. This part of the brain is responsible for complex thought, including problem solving, planning, organization, impulse control, timing, attention, and concentration, etc. When we are engaged in complex thought, the blood in the brain is concentrated in the frontal lobe—the ideal mode of operating unless under imminent threat. When we engage our frontal lobe, we *respond* to incoming stimuli. In contrast, when our midbrain is activated, we *react* to incoming stimuli—sometimes like an animal, as this is indeed our primitive brain.

When the brain detects threat or is simply "triggered" through any one of our senses, we metaphorically flip our lid and operate in the midbrain. The midbrain activates our survival mode, which helps us to react quickly and effectively in life-threatening situations. Survival mode requires a transfer of blood flow from the frontal lobe to the midbrain. As you know, operating in survival mode when there is not an actual threat is damaging to our physical health, as the neurochemical cocktail of chaos deteriorates our cellular functions over time.

When we are angry or in a high emotional state our lid metaphorically flips, and the midbrain is activated. This is not the ideal time to make important decisions because the intelligent part of your brain (frontal lobe) is disengaged. Do not act when your lid is flipped, because such actions can cause serious harm to yourself and others. Most suicides and homicides occur when the midbrain takes over. Moreover, do not engage someone whose "lid is flipped"—allow them to cool down.

How do you close your lid? You need to take a time-out and cool down to let the blood return to your frontal lobe (cerebral cortex). This takes approximately 30 minutes. And of course, deep breathing works like a charm when our intention is to reengage our frontal lobe.

Primary and secondary emotions

Ralph spends the first half of the movie *Wreck-It Ralph* consumed by a secondary emotion that keeps him stuck on autopilot. As you know, we cannot create or make positive and productive change when we are stuck in robot mode. When Ralph becomes aware of his emotional experience through his interactions with Vanellope, he makes peace with his primary emotion, which sets him free from the secondary emotions that have kept him stuck for so long. What are these cryptic primary and secondary emotions that I am alluding to?

Research on emotions suggests that there are two types of emotions that we experience: primary and secondary emotions. Recall that thoughts are the language of the brain and that emotions are the language of the body. Primary emotions are the raw and immediate feeling we get after an experience. It is the brain's production of chemicals that is sent throughout the body, and how we instantaneously and physically experience it is our primary emotion. Primary emotions typically include sadness, fear, disgust, joy, and surprise. They are often intense and instinctual, which makes them easy to identify. As time passes, the primary emotion fades, and we may have difficulty connecting the same emotion with the event because our mind tends to alter our perception.

Secondary emotions are the emotions that are felt after the primary emotion has been experienced. Essentially, they are the response to our primary emotion that is filtered through the mindset we choose to adopt as we analyze the experience with our frontal lobe. This filter may be our automatic thoughts, habits, or worldviews that we choose to internalize. Secondary emotions mask the sensitive and very vulnerable primary emotions. Often, secondary emotions mute and manipulate the negative primary emotions to numb or disconnect us from a psychologically painful experience. Some of the secondary emotions can result in more hurt and pain as they build up over time, especially if they are emotions such as shame, frustration, regret, and guilt. These emotions may be programmed into us during our childhood. Our programs have emotional algorithms or social rules to abide by, dictating how we "should" feel. Can you guess what Ralph's primary and secondary emotions could be?

Many cultures create an ideal image of a man and how a man "should" experience emotions. These cultures may convey that men "should" not demonstrate emotional weakness. We see this play out in Ralph's scenario. It is evident that Ralph's initial rejection by the Nicelanders causes him deep emotional hurt that is grounded in sadness and maybe even fear of rejection. Because Ralph plays a masculine role, he may feel that it is not appropriate for him to show sadness or fear.

Instead, he transforms his primary emotions into something that is socially more acceptable, like anger and frustration. Ralph is fortunate to have found a friend that confronts him with love when he musters the courage to reveal his most authentic and vulnerable self. The only way to liberate negative emotional energy is to make peace with the truth attached to your primary emotion.

Secondary emotions are expressed over primary emotions when we feel threatened, overwhelmed, or unsafe. Behaviors congruent with secondary emotions may include criticism, attacks, blame, withdrawal, and resentment. Again, these are protective behaviors that prevent our true feelings from being exposed. Remember, it is the truth that sets us free. The more we keep masking our truth, the more difficult it is to heal, and the gateway to healing is vulnerability. Remember, those who truly love you will accept your truth and treasure your vulnerability—just as you would do the same for them. Don't let your gnarly secondary emotions hinder you—set them free, so that you can take back your creative energy!

Process Questions

- ➤ Do you depend too much upon your external environment to be the source of your joy?

  - o If so, what things or people do you depend on?

- ➤ What secondary emotions are keeping you stuck?
- ➤ What is the primary emotion to these secondary emotions?
- ➤ What sort of mental filters might you be using to create your secondary emotions?
- ➤ Are these mental filters serving you in a good way?
- ➤ What is preventing you from being vulnerable to yourself and those closest to you?
- ➤ How can vulnerability help you find your own freedom?
- ➤ What old and unhealthy behaviors can you replace?

  - o What new and healthy behaviors should you replace them with?

Freedom Rhythm

- ➤ Please turn to page 180 to read about Freedom Rhythm and how to perform it.
- ➤ **Transformation Zone 3:**

  - o **Visualization with bilateral stimulation:** *I want you to imagine setting your truth free. In doing so, you feel spiritually, psychologically, and physically lighter!*
  - o The mindset that informs your creative movement:

    - ▪ Dedicated Decision: "I AM truthful."
    - ▪ Fantastic Feeling: "Freedom and release."

  - o Positive Affirmation: "I AM truthful! Yes, I AM!" x 3

PART IV: TRANSFORMATION

Illustration of
John Campbell's
Hero's Journey

Return

Call to Adventure

Supernatural aid

Known

Unknown

Threshold
(beginning of
transformation)

Atonement

The Hero's Journey

Mentor

Helper

Challenges and Temptations

Transformation   REVELATION

Death &
Rebirth

Helper

Chapter 9

REWRITE IT. REWIRE IT.

"All the adversity I've had in my life, all my troubles and obstacles, have strengthened me. You may not realize it when it happens, but a kick in the teeth may be the best thing in the world for you."

WALT DISNEY

I T IS TRULY IMPOSSIBLE for us to create to our fullest potential and to live our divine design for our divine destiny when we are spiritually and psychologically traumatized. For the purpose of this book, trauma will be defined as a painful experience that has negatively impacted the way we see ourselves, others, and the world at large. It is an experience that is grounded in one of the many facets of fear and imprisons us in the fear program. A traumatic event can steal our "I AM" and leave us believing, *I'm not enough.*

The highest grossing Disney movie of all time, and one of the most profound trauma recovery stories of the century, is *The Lion King.* We create stories for every life experience—it is a way of learning and evolving. But not all stories are created equal. Some stories set us free, while other stories hold us captive, sometimes for a lifetime. We get so caught up in the story that we forget that we are the author.

In the Pride Lands of Africa, lions rule and reign over the animal kingdom from Pride Rock. The valiant and noble King, Mufasa, teaches his young son Simba about the responsibilities of kingship and the harmonious circle of life. Mufasa explains to Simba, "Everything you see exists together in a delicate balance. While others search for what they can take, a true king searches for what he can give." Simba relishes in his father's wisdom and abundant love, and eagerly anticipates taking the throne when he is grown. Simba shares his childhood with his best friend Nala, to whom he is later betrothed. Nala is a fiery spirit who challenges Simba in a playful and competitive way—keeping him on his toes.

Behind the scenes, Scar, Mufasa's younger brother, covets the throne and plots the death of his brother and nephew. Scar forms an alliance with the greedy hyenas, who are banned from the territory because of their insatiable appetites and utter disregard for the circle of life. Scar sets up a trap and lures Simba into a gorge, convincing him that it has the best acoustics for practicing his roar. Scar encourages Simba to gift his father with his roar as reconciliation for being disobedient. Moreover, he tells Simba that this is the location where his father used to practice his roar. Once Simba is in place, Scar signals the hyenas to drive a large herd of wildebeest into a stampede to trample him in the gorge.

Scar urgently informs Mufasa of Simba's endangerment, in hopes that he will rush to rescue him. Mufasa heroically saves Simba but has difficulty exiting the gorge by climbing the steep and rocky ledge. After intense physical struggle, Mufasa makes it to the top of the ledge where Scar is waiting. He asks for his brother's assistance to climb over. Scar approaches him, but instead of helping, Scar shoves Mufasa off the ledge, as Simba watches his father fall hundreds of feet to his death.

Scar manipulates the mind of the small cub and writes his story, making Simba the unforgiveable villain. This is the dialogue between Scar and Simba, as Simba mourns over the body of his deceased father:

Scar: "Simba, what have you done?"

Simba: "It was a stampede. He tried to save me—it was an accident. I didn't mean for it to..."

Scar: "Of course, you didn't. No one ever means for these things to happen, but the King is dead, and if it weren't for you, he'd still be alive. Your father had such hopes for you, gave you so many chances, and this is how you repay him? What would your mother think? A son who causes his father's death. A boy who kills a King. Run, run away, Simba. Run away and never return!"

Scar orders the hyenas to kill Simba, but he escapes and wanders into the savannas of Africa, where he is rescued by Pumba and Timon (Warthog and Meerkat). There, he is taught to embrace a carefree lifestyle that is embodied in the phrase "hakuna-matata," which means "no worries." Simba is filled with shame and does not speak about the tragic past that he has buried deep inside his soul. In the meantime, death and disease are rapidly consuming the Pride Land, as Scar's gluttonous rule alongside the hyenas has destroyed the delicate balance of the circle of life. Nala escapes in search of help and is surprised when she finds Simba living in the outskirts, as Scar told the pride that he was dead.

Simba and Nala fall in love, and she encourages him to rescue Pride Rock and rightfully take back his throne so that their kingdom can thrive once more. Simba experiences spiritual warfare wherein his "I'm," which is buried in lies and shame, battles his "I AM"—*his true and highest self—a king like his father.* A mystic monkey, named Rafiki, shows him his father in his reflection in the water. In this magical experience, the storm clouds reveal the spirit of his father that speaks loving and healing words over Simba, giving him the peace and closure that he needs to rightfully take back his throne and restore his kingdom. Simba realizes that the spirit of Mufasa is inside of him.

Simba returns to Pride Rock with Nala and musters the courage to reveal the truth about Mufasa's death. Scar brags about killing Mufasa, which enrages the pride of lions, who then attack Scar and the hyenas. Simba confronts Scar, who blames all the havoc on the hyenas and urges that they be put to death. Scar begs for his life to be spared. Compassionate to the interloper, Simba tells Scar to run and to never return. Scar unexpectedly lashes out at Simba and falls from the edge of a cliff. When Scar comes to, he is surrounded by the hyenas, who overhead the conversation he had with Simba. The leader of the hyenas tells Scar, "There is only one true thing you've ever said, Scar. A hyena's belly is never full."

Simba rewrites his story—a story that is grounded in love and truth—a story that sets him free—a story that inspires hope and healing—a story that restores harmony—a story that gives life. It's time for you to do the same. Let's rewrite the story that imprisons you, and extinguish the fires of shame, guilt, remorse, and regret. We all deserve a story wherein we are the hero, or wherein we *become* the hero to embrace a new beginning.

Why do bad things happen?

Let us entertain an existential view on the topic of pain and suffering that has the possibility to set us free. At this point, you have solidly grasped that love is the divine and eternal source of all things. This may prompt you to ask if love is the source, why is there so much pain and suffering in our lives and throughout the world?

First and foremost, love does not cause pain and suffering. There is no fear or selfishness in love. Love does not exist all by itself in a vacuum or silo. Love can only be experienced through connection which forms a relationship wherein love is found. It may be our connection to the source, love itself, or it may be a connection to others.

To have a relationship, you must have free will to decide whether that relationship will be formed in the first place. This is the order of prerequisites: *Free Will→ Relationship→Love.* The bottom line is that love is freedom: It never forces; it only flows. You cannot have love without free will. If our free will were displayed as a spectrum of choices, one end of the spectrum would be *love*, and at the opposite end would be *fear.* If you recall, we are choosing to attach ourselves to either the love program or the fear program. People demonstrate their fear through acts of selfishness and cruelty as they choose to pass on the energetic hurt that they have received from someone else. Love is not the author of hurt or the bad things that we encounter in life.

Because we are alive, suffering is inevitable. No one is immune to the suffering of this world—not even the most revered spiritual persons in all of history (Jesus, Buddha, Mohammed, etc.). Moreover, Disney movies as you know them would not exist if their characters didn't experience their own type of suffering and existential struggle. It is all part of the Hero's Journey wherein we discover the depth of our incredible "I AM."

Painful experiences fall into one of two categories: *loss*, which includes death and destruction, and—you guessed it—the *selfish* or cruel acts of others that stem from fear. At times we have been at the receiving end of someone's wickedness—at other times, we have been the source of it. Many people don't recognize the tremendous power in the silent choice of whether to transfer the energetic hurt they have received to someone else or to transform it into something good.

If everything is energy, and energy cannot be created nor destroyed, only transformed or transferred, what does that mean about life and death? Perhaps Mufasa is right when he speaks to Simba from the clouds, many years after his death: *I never left you. I never will. Remember who you are.* We are all connected through the divine power and energy of love that cannot be destroyed. Our bodies are temporary vessels for our "I AM," and our "I AM" is everlasting.

Nietzsche said, "The meaninglessness of suffering, not suffering itself, was the curse that lay over mankind." He's right! If the story you've created around your suffering is meaningless or grounded in self-hatred, it is indeed a curse. Only you can rewrite your story to have profound purpose grounded in growth, learning, and love. It's up to you to turn your trials and tribulations into testimonies or your problems into power. After all, you are the creator.

Psychological wounds

I would much prefer to have a deep physical wound than a deep psychological wound caused by a painful life experience. A psychological wound, if not properly treated, can persist for a lifetime. It can completely rewire your brain and your perception of yourself, others, and the world—if you allow it to. A psychological wound may trigger a person to operate in the fear program wherein the neurochemical cocktail of chaos constantly floods their body, downregulating their genes for premature death and disease. But the good news is that if you know how to rewrite your trauma narrative (story), you can rewire your brain!

Like an infected wound, your psychological and spiritual wounds must be treated. The infection is like a poison that threatens to spread throughout your body. It MUST be removed. Recalling the painful memory is like reopening the wound to clean it out—it's no fun. Though this pain is intense, it is only temporary. It's better to embrace the temporary pain than endure a lifetime of rotting from the inside out. Once the wound is cleaned and healed, you are left with a scar. The story you tell about your scar will determine the outcome of your spiritual and psychological healing, so create a meaningful narrative that is filled with hope to inspire others to heal. Your freedom is found in the story you tell.

The only way out is through

Vulnerability is the gateway to healing. You cannot heal without passing through the arches of vulnerability to eventually embrace self-acceptance for the good, the bad, and the ugly. To return to his throne, Simba absolutely had to confront every detail of his painful past. The truth came to light, as it always does, and it set him free.

Why do we fear vulnerability? Because it requires us to confront our shame. Shame is a device contrived by the fear program. We are shameful because we fear we are not enough. Shame holds our most precious relationships hostage. *Would you still love me if you really knew me? Or what I did?* As humans, we all experience shame, some more than others, depending upon the programs we have downloaded. Simba felt shameful and feared that if Nala knew his truth she would no longer love him, but that was not the case—not even close!

In life there are consequences for everything: "You reap what you sow." Life is a good punisher—recall that her name is Karma; she works hand in hand with the laws of forgiveness, harmony, and grace. The law of karma confirms that your perpetrator will never get away with the hurt they caused you, whether it is punished by law or not. What you put out into the universe—good or bad—is what comes back to you and sometimes it's multiplied. If you were once a perpetrator, I'm sure you have felt the consequences emotionally, physically, and psychologically of the hurt that you have caused. In fact, the sooner you break down the barriers of shame and acknowledge your truth by letting love in and asking for spiritual forgiveness by demonstrating that you have learned from your mistakes, the sooner harmony and grace can come to your rescue. They are eager rescuers!

There is no rule that states we must punish ourselves. In fact, how are we able to fully reach our potential to make the world better if we are punishing and shaming ourselves? How much energy does self-punishment and shame consume that could instead be used toward improving the collective conscience of the world? Moreover, self-punishment is self-inflicted emotional pain that causes us to hurt. If people who are hurting hurt other people, then it is likely you will unintentionally release your emotional hurt on the ones closest to you. It is our responsibility to stop the cycle of hurting. Self-punishment is your decision to unnecessarily torment yourself. Do not be imprisoned by your own mind—choose freedom! You are not alone in your experience, and you are not the first person to have felt how you feel. Do not give shame and self-loathing the ink and pen to write the story of your life!

Confronting the painful past

You may think that your brain is a real "nuisance" every time it allows an intrusive and traumatic memory to resurface into your conscious awareness. Well, you're wrong. Believe it or not, your brain is trying to do you a favor! It's creating an extraction site to release the poison that is contaminating your entire being—but you keep shoving the poison back down because you don't want to deal with it. The more you shove it down the more toxic it becomes. Your traumatic memories are like a poison that your brain is trying to extract, just as a splinter is a foreign object that your body naturally pushes to the surface for removal. Your avoidance is the problem! In fact, avoidance is the hallmark trait of post-traumatic stress, and it exacerbates the rest of your trauma symptoms (hypervigilance, nightmares, intrusive memories, negative thoughts/emotions). Allow the extraction site to be an extraction site, not a graveyard to continue burying the poison.

People tend to remember unfinished, unresolved, or interrupted tasks better than completed ones. This psychological experience is called the Zeigarnik effect. Why does this happen? Because your brain was designed to operate on the wavelength of love and peace, not fear and chaos. Your brain yearns for completion and closure, so it draws your attention to what is incomplete so that you may complete it. When you complete it, by rescripting your trauma narrative, you will have peace, not only in your mind, but in every single cell in your body.

Psychological indigestion

My son loves the old movie, *Like Mike,* which can be found on Disney Plus. It's about a young boy whose magic basketball shoes give him the ability to do the impossible on the basketball court. His skills are so phenomenal that he is drafted at the age of twelve into the NBA. As an orphan, the lead character Calvin is in awe of the opulent lifestyle lived by the NBA players. During his first away game, Calvin marvels at the grandeur of his hotel and discovers the room service menu. He orders and consumes all the junk food available, passes out in a food coma, and when he comes to, he experiences projectile vomiting during the most inopportune time. Have you ever had a binge fest? I have. It's all fun and games until the pyrotechnics of indigestion kick in and force the food out of you from one of two ends, or both at the same time!!! Bottom line—junk food binges are a traumatic event to your gut.

You and those around you notice the effects of your indigestion. In contrast, healthy food in moderation doesn't cause indigestion. Instead, your body extracts the nutrients, and you *dump* what you don't need—pun totally intended. The brain operates in the same way. A traumatic experience results in psychological indigestion, while typical experiences—like running an errand to the grocery store or remembering where you parked while you were there—are filed in our short-term memory and then dumped (forgotten) if not needed.

In contrast, our painful and traumatic memories are filed away in the emotion center of your brain known as the limbic system. If your memory evokes the emotion of fear, it is filed away in the amygdala—the area of the brain responsible for activating your survival response. Let's go back to the analogy of your brain as a computer and your mind as a software program. Traumatic memories are saved in *high definition*, creating memories that incorporate your five senses that keep record of your triggers. As you know, saving high-definition content takes up more space on your hard drive, and if filled with too much of such content, the hard drive reaches its capacity or crashes. This results in poor memory. You may also notice that the only emotion you are capable of experiencing is anger. That's because your emotional storage capacity is also full. How do you fix that? You process the files and save them in a different format—one that frees up space. Do you notice how often I use the term freedom in one way or another? Recovering from trauma is all about finding a way to set ourselves free!

Healing the brain through the mind

How do we process painful memories? We must examine the narrative we've created for our memory. If we've identified ourselves as the villain in the story, we need to seriously rethink the circumstances through an objective lens. Painful experiences have the tendency to uproot our view of ourselves, others, the world, and our faith—if we allow them. When our experiences do not line up with our long-held beliefs, we feel anxiety. To manage this anxiety, we begin to twist the narrative in our memory to experience relief. This twisted thinking is often our worst enemy. It's easier to blame ourselves than to blame others, because we can control ourselves. Traumatic experiences steal your control. Many people cope with trauma by overexerting control over every aspect of their life. This is exhausting and damaging to our health and our most precious relationships, though it is an attempt to feel safe in a world in which our traumatic experience left us feeling powerless. In contrast, Simba chooses to give up control and to live a carefree life, another ineffective way of coping that falls on the opposite end of the spectrum of control. His loss of control made him feel apathetic, as he would rather "not care" than risk being hurt once more. Of course, Simba moved past this phase of coping before taking the throne.

Simba was stuck on blaming himself for the death of his father and the ruin of the Pride Lands because of Scar's ravenous reign. As a small cub at the time of his father's death, Simba was easily manipulated into believing a radical lie. Simba's shame was so great that he never stopped to revisit the story that Scar programmed into his mind. Let's review what transpired: *Scar sets up a trap and lures Simba into a gorge, convincing him that it has the best acoustics for practicing his roar. Scar encourages Simba to gift his father with his roar as reconciliation for being disobedient. Moreover, he tells Simba that this is the location where his father used to practice his roar. Once Simba is in place, Scar signals the hyenas to drive a large herd of wildebeest into a stampede to trample him in the gorge.*

If I were in a therapy session with Simba, I'd ask him a few questions to help him get unstuck. This sort of questioning is called Socratic questioning, as it works to challenge our dysfunctional beliefs. My conversation with Simba might go something like this...

> ➤ *Simba, as a child, were you taught to respect your elders?*

> ○ **Yes.**

> ➤ *As a child, were you encouraged to trust your family?*

> ○ **Absolutely.**

> ➤ *As a child, did you believe that the elders in your family always had your best interest at heart?*

> ○ **I did.**

> ➤ *As a child, was a powerful roar important to you?*

> ○ **Very important.**

➤ *As a child, did you wish to be like your father?*

   ○ **Yes, I still do.**

➤ *As a child, did you wish to please your father?*

   ○ **Always.**

➤ *As a child, did you think it was safe to take the advice of your uncle?*

   ○ **Yes.**

➤ *Prior to the traumatic event, did your uncle harm you in any way?*

   ○ **Never. He was just grumpy.**

➤ *As a child, were you instructed to steer clear of your uncle?*

   ○ **No.**

➤ *As a child, did you have any reason not to trust your uncle?*

   ○ **Unfortunately, no. He just seemed like a miserable and cranky old lion.**

➤ *If you had a crystal ball to predict the future that day, what would you have done differently?*

   ○ **Everything! I would have avoided my uncle and informed my father of his evil intentions. I would have done everything in my power to protect my father and myself from his evil plotting.**

➤ *Considering the answers to your questions, what would you say to that young cub now?*

   ○ **Simba, you trusted your uncle who you believed had your best interest at heart. Your intention to "gift" your** father with your roar was genuine and sincere. You always wanted to make your father proud. You obeyed your uncle because you were never instructed otherwise. There was no way of knowing what would transpire in the gorge. I'm sorry you had to endure so much pain and suffering—you deserved so much better.

➢ *This is what your uncle said to you immediately after your father's death:*

    ○ *"... but the King is dead, and if it weren't for you, he'd still be alive. Your father had such hopes for you, gave you so many chances, and this is how you repay him? What would your mother think? A son who causes his father's death. A boy who kills a King. Run, run away, Simba. Run away and never return!"*

➢ *What do you have to say in return?*

    ○ "Scar, you are weak and pathetic to have preyed on an innocent cub and then turn your back on your brother when he needed you. You are not deserving of my energy." In fact, I told Scar to run away—exactly what he said to me. I chose not to end his life, because I refused to be like him. You reap what you sow. Ironically, he experienced exactly what he did to me, and so much worse when the hyenas had their way. He was a sad and pathetic soul and I refuse to attach any of my precious energy to him. I release him from my energy field.

➢ *That is powerful. Now, I want you to close your eyes and find your father. What do you need to say to him? And what do you need to hear from him? Stay in this visualization for as long as you need... When you are through, please tell me what you experienced.*

    ○ My father is larger than life in Heaven. His love poured over me and provided unexplainable comfort. Before I could get a word in, he said, "Son, I am proud of you. I am sorry for what you had to endure. I am sorry that you felt alone. I am sorry that I didn't know the depths of your uncle's darkness. I have always been with you—and now you know how to find me. You are my greatest legacy—and you have surpassed me in all ways. I am a part of everything you see in the great circle of life. I love you forever." That's all I needed to hear. I didn't have to say a word—there was no need. I am at peace.

➢ *Let's do a "before and after" story. What was your old narrative?*

    ○ Once upon a time, there was an ornery lion cub named Simba. He killed his father the great king and was banished from the lands because he was a murderer—a disappointment to all. This lion cub was rescued by other animal species because they pitied him and thought he was pathetic. If they only knew his truth, they would disown him immediately. Simba grew into a weak and apathetic lion who lived miserably ever after and cared about nothing.

➢ *Now, what is your new narrative?*

    ○ Once upon a time, there was a beautiful lion cub named Simba. He had a zest for life and adventure and wanted nothing more than to become a great king like his father. Simba was manipulated into dangerous situations by his jealous uncle, who took advantage of his naivete and sought to murder him and his father. Trusting in his family, Simba innocently took the advice of his uncle with the intention of making his father proud. Little did Simba know that this advice was a trap and coup to overthrow the entire animal kingdom. The evil uncle convinced Simba that he was responsible for his father's death—though there was nothing further from the truth. Simba was instructed to run away, and he obeyed. Simba

was brave and survived many of his uncle's attempts to end his life. He thrived with newfound friends and a new outlook because he was resilient. Simba didn't want to be an emotional burden, so he buried his pain and suffered in silence. When Simba encountered his long-lost friend Nala, he listened with an open heart to her pleas. Simba bravely confronted the fears of his past to rescue his family and the animal kingdom from his uncle's terror. Simba was even more courageous to show his uncle compassion by sparing his life. The truth of his uncle's evil coup was revealed, and Simba was spiritually set free. He ruled and reigned with more love, compassion, and generosity than any king before him. Simba and all the animals in his kingdom lived happily ever after in the circle of life.

Look at all that we imagined together!!! You literally imagined me in a therapy session with a lion! I love it. The power of our imagination is limitless.

Are you getting the hang of how I helped Simba get unstuck? I started with a series of questions that proved Simba could not predict the future, and that there was no evidence to assume a radical coup of this magnitude was about to transpire. Moreover, I emphasized that each one of Simba's actions came from a place of love and respect for his father.

One of my favorite techniques as a clinical psychologist is asking my patients to visualize a scene in their mind that they believe will help bring them peace. This scene does not contribute to the chaos that is already present in their minds, and violence is never the answer. Simba chose to visualize his father in Heaven. Recall that your brain does not know the difference between a real and an imagined experience. The mind tricks the brain into obtaining the closure that it needs. However, you can also see this as a form of spiritual closure, as we ground our healing visualization in pure love.

Did you notice how short Simba's "before" narrative was? This is truly a perfect example of the oversimplification we create when formulating our initial trauma narratives. Moreover, it comes from a place of haste because of our desire to avoid sitting with the unpleasant memory long enough to objectively dissect it. The energy of Simba's new narrative was derived from the love program, inspiring hope, and healing.

To lay down an adaptive neural network in his brain, Simba should read his new trauma narrative at least twice a day for 33 consecutive days, to ensure that his new narrative overrides his old one. Are you realizing that this is not rocket science? You have the power to create the healing within you. Now it's your turn—after all, you were born to create!

Process Questions

- ➤ What will happen to you if you speak your truth to yourself?
- ➤ What if you speak it to someone who loves you?
- ➤ Without the use of violence, how can you rescript your painful experience to bring you peace?
- ➤ What do you regret? Can you turn this regret into a lesson? What is the lesson?
- ➤ You didn't have a crystal ball to predict the future, so what thought do you need to realize to let yourself off the hook?
- ➤ Do you harbor shame? Why?
- ➤ Do you harbor fear of vulnerability? Why?
- ➤ Can you think of a time when you were loving and compassionate to someone who was vulnerable with you and who overcame their shame in your presence?
- ➤ How did it feel to receive that vulnerability?

Freedom Rhythm

- ➤ Please turn to page 180 to read about Freedom Rhythm and how to perform it.
- ➤ <u>**Transformation Zone 3:**</u>

  - o **<u>Visualization with bilateral stimulation:</u>** *I want you to rehearse your new narrative—one grounded in love and truth. Allow yourself to become the hero in your new narrative, as we all deserve a second chance.*
  - o <u>The mindset that informs your creative movement:</u>

    - ▪ <u>Dedicated Decision:</u> "I AM the hero."
    - ▪ <u>Fantastic Feeling:</u> "Child-like excitement."

  - o <u>Positive Affirmation:</u> "I AM the hero! Yes, I AM!" x 3

Chapter 10

EXTRACTING THE POISON

"I always like to look on the optimistic side of life, but I am realistic enough to know that life is a complex matter."

WALT DISNEY

"**W**ELL, WE JUST COMPLETED A therapy session with a lion. How do you feel about that?" I ask in my most therapeutic tone. Now let's see if it works on a human! Let's invite Elsa—from Disney's 2013 feature film *Frozen*—to sit back, relax, and enjoy the therapeutic ride on a shrink's sofa. Elsa has experienced multiple traumatic events throughout her lifetime. Let's identify these events and figure out how to help Elsa get unstuck from the *fear program* by doing brain surgery— not really, but close!

Princess Elsa of Arendelle has magical powers that allow her to control snow and ice to create magnificent structures, control the weather, and even bring to life an adorable snowman named Olaf. Elsa and Anna are sisters, who spend the days of their childhood entertaining themselves with Elsa's magic. While playing, Elsa accidentally strikes Anna with her magical force. Devastated, Elsa and her parents seek healing and guidance from Grand Pabbie, the ruler of the trolls. After healing Anna and removing her memories of Elsa's magical gifting, his advice to Elsa is this:

> "Listen to me, Elsa. Your power will only grow. There is beauty in it, and also great danger. You must learn to control it—fear will be your enemy." Elsa's father replies to his guidance, "We will protect her. She can learn to control it, I'm sure. Until then, we lock the gates, we'll reduce the staff, we will limit her contact with people, and keep her powers hidden from everyone, including Anna."

As you can imagine, Elsa was deeply saddened and terrified to receive this news. She locked herself away for many years. Compounding her grief, Elsa's parents died in a shipwreck. At the age of twenty-one, Elsa is to become queen of Arendelle. Her greatest concern is that her subjects will discover her magic and fear her, just as she fears herself. During the first public gathering in years, hosted by Queen Elsa, Anna publicly pleads with Elsa to marry a man she literally just met. Elsa refuses to bless their union, which prompts Anna to inquire about Elsa's self-isolation and cold demeanor. Infuriated by Anna's public interrogation, Elsa's anger and fear trigger the release of her magic, and ice is weaponized against the crowd as a form of self-defense. Humiliated, Elsa runs for the mountains and creates her own winter wonderland, a magical ice castle wherein she plans to isolate herself indefinitely.

Unbeknownst to her, Elsa has left Arendelle under a frozen spell of eternal winter. Her worst nightmare has come true, as her people are terrified of her. Moreover, she is branded a monster by the visiting dignitaries, particularly a conniving duke, who wishes to seize her throne. Anna goes in search of Elsa to urge her to undo the eternal winter and return home so that they can mend their sisterhood and their kingdom. When the two sisters reunite, Elsa is pleased to see Anna but demands that she leave and never return, as she fears her magical powers will accidentally harm her. Again, Anna pushes Elsa's limits as she professes her love for her, and in doing so, Elsa's magic is inadvertently released, accidentally striking Anna in the heart. Elsa creates an ice monster to force Anna out of her castle, as she fears that she will do more harm than good.

Now as an adult, Anna visits Grand Pabbie once again. He is unable to cure her frozen heart, which will soon result in death unless an *"act of true love"* reverses the spell. In the meantime, the duke captures Elsa in her frozen castle and holds her prisoner in Arendelle. Anna is rapidly growing weaker, and death is imminent. Anna believes that a kiss from any one of the men she shared romantic feelings with is the answer to undoing the curse that plagues her freezing heart. Elsa escapes her prison cell and rushes to reach Anna before it is too late.

In a climactic uproar, Anna is nearing her end as she searches to receive a kiss from Kristoff, her new friend and most recent crush. With the intention of seizing her throne, the duke searches for Elsa, planning to end her life because of Anna's death—though she has not yet died. Anna sees Kristoff approaching her in the distance but is distracted by Elsa, whose back is turned to the duke, who has his sword drawn over her. In a flash, Anna must decide if she will save herself from the icy death that is drawing nearer or save her sister from the blade.

As the duke raises his sword, Anna comes between it and her sister. When the sword comes barreling down, it strikes a frozen Anna, who takes her final breath. Elsa turns around to see her sister frozen in an act of true heroism. Elsa mourns over her sister, who begins to defrost.

> Elsa asks Anna, "You sacrificed yourself for me?" Olaf replies, "An act of true love will unthaw a frozen heart." Excitement pours over Elsa, and she proclaims, "Love, of course, Elsa! Love!!!"

Elsa's greatest epiphany is finally realizing that love is the key to controlling her magic. Elsa dispels the eternal winter, beautifies her kingdom with fabulous ice structures, and celebrates with her subjects on an ice-skating rink. Olaf is given a magical flurry cloud so that he may endure all climates. The duke is banished from Arendelle for treason. The sisters are reunited in love and harmony, and they live happily ever after until *Frozen II.*

The fear program & trauma

Trauma is rooted deeply in the fear program, creating chaos and disharmony in our hearts and minds that eventually spills over into our 3D reality. It is imperative to understand that fear and negative energy only attract more fear and negative energy. Grand Pabbie explains it best: "Listen to me, Elsa. Your power will only grow. There is beauty in it, and also great danger. You must learn to control it—fear will be your enemy." Fear also has an electromagnetic signature that communicates with the universe, and it is also capable of manifestation through the law of attraction. The more you fear something, the more you attract it. This is why Elsa could not harness her powers. She was so afraid of losing control that she lost control. We must do our very best to ensure that every intention comes from the love program. *There is no fear in love, but perfect love casts out all fear (John 4:18).*

Let it go!!!—Queen Elsa

I would be the richest woman on the planet if I received a dollar for every time a patient told me that they felt it was best for their hurtful experiences to remain buried in the past. Most people don't want to confront the past to find peace and healing. They would rather endure the pain of burying the poison than endure the short-lived fear of confronting it, to "let it go" and finally be free.

Let's stick with the snow theme. Think about a snowball. The hurt and pain of a traumatic event starts off the size of a snowball. You have the option to shatter the snowball immediately by emotionally digesting the impact of the event on your life, or you can ignore it. When you ignore it, the snowball keeps rolling downhill, growing larger and larger until it becomes an avalanche capable of being set off by the slightest of triggers. Your desire to avoid the painful past is human nature; hence, the symptom of avoidance has become known as the hallmark trait of post-traumatic stress.

I think Elsa has it wrong. She sings about her desire to "let it go" to be set free. However, the magnitude of her pain and suffering is not something that "let it go" can fix without some serious psychological and spiritual processing. It would be appropriate to "let it go" as it pertains to petty bickering or a rejection letter that you felt lukewarm about to begin with.

Elsa sings "let it go!" as she is running from her problems and her fear of controlling her magical powers. Even after singing her heart out about "letting it go," she continues to operate in the fear program, believing that self-isolation and abandonment of her kingdom are the answers to her problems. Elsa's "let it go" is very much like Simba's "hakuna matata!" Moreover, when Anna visits her in the ice castle, Elsa still wants to avoid the problem. In fact, she encourages Anna to also run away from the dysfunction that is tearing apart their sisterhood and their kingdom. In life, you pick and choose what is a "let it go!" situation vs not. Some things are worth fighting for, like your sisterhood and your kingdom. Sometimes the fight is internal, as our "I AM" battles our "I'm not enough" until only one is left standing. When your problem is solved by *love and truth* then you can "let it go" and be free. But if your problem is still answered by fear and chaos, you have work to do before you can just "let it go!"

Elsa's Christmas tree star

If you have several traumatic life experiences that you have yet to confront for the purpose of healing, addressing only one trauma in isolation will trigger all of them. You cannot extract one trauma independent of all the others because they are all interconnected. The good news is this: You have likely created a trauma theme for each of your traumatic experiences. This means that once you unravel one maladaptive trauma narrative, you have likely unraveled the others. Psychologists generally always begin trauma treatment on the topic of the most emotionally painful experience because it has the greatest positive effect. Think of it like the star at the top of the Christmas tree. Once it is lit, it casts light over the entire tree. If you only turn on one light toward the bottom of the tree, it will only cast light on the part of the tree that is below it. Since we always want to get the most "bang for our buck," we start with the most painful traumatic experience—like the star at the top of the Christmas tree. This is called maximizing our efforts through the most effective and efficient means available. Trust me, we want to operate as swiftly as possible. Elsa's star goes all the way back to childhood, wherein she was locked away in her room to protect the kingdom from her magical powers.

Trauma & control

Let's examine some thinking traps that prevent us from healing after traumatic experiences. Control is a major theme when it comes to trauma recovery because traumatic experiences typically cause us to feel powerless and out of control. After surviving a traumatic event, most people long to reestablish their control to feel safe. This often results in stress and frustration as we try to micromanage our lives and the lives of those we love. The sooner we can accept that we can't control everything, the sooner the healing process begins.

Look at what Elsa's parents did after the accident caused by her magic. "We will protect her. She can learn to control it, I'm sure. Until then, we lock the gates, we'll reduce the staff, we will limit her contact with people, and keep her powers hidden from everyone, including Anna." Does that behavior sound like control? Absolutely! Do you think this sort of reaction helped Elsa to accept her powers through love and truth? Absolutely not! This sort of controlling behavior made Elsa fear her powers even more. It may have also made her feel like a monster who needed to be locked away from the world.

The only true control we have is over our *internal experiences*, which are our own reactions and perceptions to the world around us— essentially, that includes our thoughts, emotions, and behaviors. Only you can decide how you will respond to the environment around you.

Second, no one has control over *external experiences*, which include the behaviors, thoughts, and emotions of others. Some of us feel stuck on situations or events over which we had no external control. We falsely convince ourselves that we had control over the painful outcomes of awful life events because it is easier to blame ourselves than to come to the hard realization that we can be subjected to terrible circumstances that are not within our control.

Control over external experiences implies we are 100% responsible for the outcome of a situation—but that statement couldn't be further from the truth. Instead, we have _influence_ over external experiences. Our own influence over these experiences ranges from _low to high_. In most bad situations, our influence is limited. I address the topic of influence vs. control to free us from holding ourselves hostage to the belief that we should take sole responsibility for every bad thing that has happened in our life. When we choose to own such heavy responsibility, we become slaves to emotions of guilt and shame.

Elsa could not control the fact that she was born with magical powers. Moreover, she did not have anyone who could teach her how to harness her powers for good. Elsa never intended to harm anyone, though she harbored unrelenting guilt for the accidents caused by her magical powers. The only thing Elsa believed she had control over was her exposure to the world and that is why she isolated herself from it— for the protection of others.

Prisoner of twisted guilt

You feel guilty because you feel you could've/should've "done more," or you should've "known better" to prevent X, Y, or Z from happening. I coined a term for this type of convoluted self-blame—_twisted guilt._ It occurs when you falsely convince yourself that you were in 100% _control of external experiences._ Remember, we NEVER have control of external events—only _influence_ over them. You cannot hold your past self accountable for what you know now. That is absurd! Don't get stuck holding onto the emotion of guilt, especially when it is illogical. How are you benefitting from the twisted guilt you have chosen to hold on to?

Ask yourself, am I using the "hindsight is 20/20" concept to support my twisted guilt? Hindsight is 20/20 means that we clearly see the past with perfect vision because we have learned the outcome of our decisions. How is it fair to judge your past decisions with the knowledge that you have now? It makes no sense for you to punish yourself for what you didn't know then—whether it was something that could only be acquired through experience, time, and development—or for the unforeseen and unpredictable variables caused by the external world.

Think about how the twisted guilt manifests inside of you, causing you to feel angry and irritable, so much so that your loved ones take notice. You allow this mood to dictate your thoughts, emotions, and behaviors with your family. It's likely that you act snappy, yell, or raise your voice, and brood alone in your own room. These behaviors, which stem from your twisted guilt, are all legitimate reasons to feel true guilt. The wild thing is that you allow twisted guilt to make you feel this way! Twisted guilt is a choice.

What about true guilt?

True guilt happens when we do something wrong when we have control of our *internal experience*—our thoughts, emotions, and behaviors. For example, imagine a person returning home from work after a *no good, very bad day*. When they walk into the house, their excited dog comes rushing at them, but because they're angry, they kick the dog out of way. After the emotional dust settles, this person feels guilty for being abusive toward their dog. This is *true guilt* because the person had control over their own behaviors in a non-life-threatening situation and chose to transfer their energetic hurt and frustration to an innocent bystander—their dog. Naturally, this person could've opted to behave differently. They could've taken some deep breaths or walked around the neighborhood to cool down, to ensure that their negative mood wouldn't impact others.

Essentially, it is healthy to experience true guilt or regret because we are human—imperfect and prone to making mistakes. If we never have regret, then it's essentially saying, "there was never an opportunity in my life for me to be kinder, nicer, more loving, and overall better..." Obviously, that's not true, as we can always work to operate from the love program. When we set the truth free by acknowledging our wrongs, and consciously work to improve ourselves, karma is no longer our foe. This is when we fall in line with grace and forgiveness.

Replacing guilt with self-compassion

Now that you've decided to remove your twisted guilt, absolutely do not replace it with shame. Guilt is attached to a sense of responsibility, while shame is attached to our ego and the concern about "not being good enough or being bad." Shame, though it may feel diluted, is not an acceptable emotion to replace twisted guilt. Instead, I encourage you to replace shame and guilt with self-compassion and acceptance. I'm certain that if one of your best friends approached you about their guilt and suffering related to painful life events, you would show them love and compassion. In fact, you may even try to convince them that it was not their fault. Why are you so quick to give them your compassion when you refuse to give it to yourself? Allow your compassion to be complete so that it includes those around you and, of course, yourself. Self-compassion is not weakness; it is a superpower.

Brain surgery

It's impossible to process your traumatic memories when they are imprisoned in the primitive part of your brain—the limbic system. This is where you must extract the traumatic memory from its prison and bring it to your awareness for interrogation by your frontal lobe. If you recall, the frontal lobe is the part of the brain that is capable of problem solving and engaging in complex thought.

Please remember that your memory narrative is a neural network that you have chosen to reinforce through repetition. If your memory narrative causes you distress, you must work to change it by deconstructing the old connections that bring about pain and suffering and replacing them with new connections that promote peace and healing.

For example, upon learning that a person cannot control their external environment, you may have taken a moment to contemplate how that pertains to your own traumatic experience, and then allowed yourself to feel relief from your own self-punishment. Maybe the relief lasted for a minute and then you returned to your old narrative—the maladaptive neural network that you've created. However, for the one minute that you challenged your old narrative, you weakened its neural network. When you begin to unravel the dysfunctional narrative during the interrogation process, you view it from multiple perspectives. Soon you will learn how to change your trauma narrative to one that is more accurate, more freeing, and more forgiving. This is where you delete the fear program's narrative and download the love program's narrative.

Changing your trauma narrative is like extracting the poison from it so that you may receive the antidote. When you alter the neural network of the old trauma narrative, you change the physical structure of the memory all the way down to the proteins that shape it. You will strengthen the *new* neural network by rehearsing the *new* and adaptive, healing narrative in your mind. The *healing* narrative becomes your *new* experience, and as a result, it will no longer be filed back into the amygdala (the brain's fear center), but rather filed into the regular long-term memory in the hippocampus. Now that you have extracted the poison from the trauma narrative (memory), your brain will no longer threaten you with intrusive memories.

The only creation that can think about thinking

Let's take advantage of this incredible ability and think about how we can use it to our advantage when rescripting our trauma narratives. We are the only living creation with true free will, metacognitive abilities, and multiple perspective advantage. No other species can think about thinking! This concept is called metacognition. We have the capacity to think about why we think the way we do—from recognizing our thinking patterns to dissecting our thoughts to understanding the consequences of our thinking to deciding to change our thinking to create a desired experience.

In a similar vein, multiple perspective approach is the ability to step outside of ourselves to see situations from perspectives other than our own. Because our imaginations are so powerful, we can place ourselves in the shoes of another person and experience how they may feel or think. We can even imagine what others may be thinking about us.

Don't forget about the power of creative reconceptualization! This is when we get creative and find unique and non-obvious ways to bring peace to our trauma narratives. It's all about using your incredible imagination to create the healing you need. Recall that your brain does not know the difference between a real and imagined experience, though your mind does. Use this to your advantage! Let's get creative with all sorts of visualizations to help set Elsa free!

Elsa's wild imagination

Our goal is to extract the poison from Elsa's trauma narrative. We will transform her self-perception from a monster who needs to be locked away to a dazzling queen whose love flows abundantly through her magical powers and upon the inhabitants of her kingdom.

At the end of *Frozen*, Elsa comes to the mind-blowing realization that love is the magnificent power that enables her magic to flourish. Even though she possesses this incredible insight, she still needs to heal psychologically and spiritually. As her imaginary psychologist, I would reiterate the importance of her "I AM." I would work to challenge her stuck thinking that revolves around feeling as though she is not enough. There is a good possibility that Elsa feels unworthy of the love that Anna has poured over her time and time again. Let's start with healing Elsa's inner child.

Here are some visualization prompts that I believe will bring Elsa tremendous closure—helping her to rescript her trauma outlook. This is where our imagination comes in to play. Essentially, we are healing the brain through the mind.

> ➤ *Visualization 1: Elsa, I want this current version of you—your adult self—to travel back in time to the lonely room in which you were locked away after the accident with Anna. I want you to approach this childhood version of you and tell her how much you love her. Shower this little girl, who is hurting so deeply and profoundly, with unconditional love. Let her know that you approve of her and that you are proud of her incredible strength. Validate her emotional experience.*

- o This visualization helps Elsa become whole. We do not want her to be "okay" with only her current state of being. We want her whole existence to come together harmoniously.

- ➤ *Visualization 2: Elsa, I want you to stay with that little girl for a while longer. I want you to teach her how to harness her magic through love. Go have fun with this version of you! She deserves to be a playful child after missing out on most of her childhood.*

  - o Elsa can relive her childhood through a lens of love and not fear. Showing the childhood version of herself how to harness her magic helps to extract the fear and anxiety from her trauma narrative.

- ➤ *Visualization 3: Elsa, go find the version of you that lives alone in the ice castle you created. This is the version of you that is mourning after the second accident with Anna. She needs love, too. Validate her emotions and tell her about all the good things that are about to happen to her.*

  - o Notice how we visit the aftermath of each traumatic event. In doing so, we eliminate shame, as we come to accept ourselves completely.

- ➤ *Visualization 4:* Prior to the last visualization, I would invite Anna to join in the counseling session. *Elsa, I want you to imagine stepping into Anna's existence. I want you to see her life from her eyes, from childhood to present. Anna, I want you to do the same. I want you to see Elsa's life from her eyes, starting from childhood to present.*

  - o Each sister would have the opportunity to share their unique point of view with the other. It is the truth that sets us free. Moreover, having the sisters visualize the other's existence evokes compassion—the most fertile ground for healing.

➤ *Visualization 5:* *Elsa, I want you to go find your parents in Heaven. Remember, in Heaven, your parents are part of the divine spirit of love. There is no fear in their existence. I imagine they wish they could have done things differently while they were alive. Listen to what they have to say to you. Also, take your time in sharing what you need to share with them.*

     ○ I imagine that Elsa still has a desire to receive her parents' approval. This visualization will help to bring her closure.

➤ *Bonus Visualization:* *Elsa, if there are events in your life that still lack closure, give yourself the opportunity for a "do-over." This is the moment wherein you can do the things you wish you could have done then!*

     ○ Dependent upon Elsa's healing progress, I would consider encouraging her to rescript her traumatic memories. However, this step may not be necessary, if she has already made peace with her past.

…And she was finally able to "let it go." Elsa lived happily ever after—creating the life she always imagined!

Process Questions

- ➤ Do you have a Christmas Tree Star? What is it?
- ➤ Have you noticed yourself holding on to guilt for something that you could not control?
- ➤ How do you punish yourself with the hindsight 20/20 bias?
- ➤ Write down the visualization you are going to practice that will help you to get unstuck.
- ➤ What does your painful experience look like when you change the narrative?
- ➤ Have you tried to "let it go" and did it work? If not, it may be important to invest time in creating a new narrative for your painful life experience—one that extracts the poison and is grounded in love and peace.
- ➤ Identify the person who loves you most in this world. How would they view you considering your painful experience?
- ➤ Creatively reconceptualize your painful experience.
- ➤ Do you have compassion for yourself? If not, why?
- ➤ How can you show compassion for yourself?

Freedom Rhythm

- ➤ Please turn to page 180 to read about Freedom Rhythm and how to perform it.
- ➤ **Transformation Zone 3:**

  - o **Visualization with bilateral stimulation:** *I want you to visit your old self, the version of you that did not feel worthy. I need you to shower that version of you with love and light!*
  - o The mindset that informs your creative movement:

    - ▪ Dedicated Decision: "I AM lovable."
    - ▪ Fantastic Feeling: "Love."

  - o Positive Affirmation: "I AM lovable! Yes, I AM!" x 3

PART V: ATONEMENT & RETURN

Illustration of
John Campbell's
Hero's Journey

Chapter 11

HARMONY

"You can design and create, and build the most wonderful place in the world. But it takes people to make the dream a reality."

WALT DISNEY

YOU ARE CLOSE TO COMPLETING the Hero's journey! This chapter packs a lot of punch, as it consolidates all the neurohacking gems into one sweet spot. Enhancing the collective conscience of the world starts when you conscientiously neurohack the fear program. The world as we know it is in a state of disharmony and disconnect. Fear and separation cause war and oppression. The only way to remedy this is one person at a time. Just as quickly as we can spread toxic energy, we can spread tonic energy. We must trust in love to lead the way and that starts with how we believe, which influences how we behave, which then determines who we become. When we learn to create together, the magnitude of our magic is exponentially more powerful and mind-blowing. We should try it sometime.

Humans and dragons lived harmoniously alongside one another in the beautiful and thriving lands of Kumandra. The colorful dragons blessed the people of Kumandra with the gifts of water, rain, and peace until the Druun arrived and turned every living thing in its path to stone. The Druun are mindless spirits, and I personally believe they were created by the *fear program*. And yes, the movie is *Raya and the Last Dragon*, debuting in 2021.

Before being turned to stone by the Druun, a family of dragons energetically transfers all their magic to their sister Sisu, *entrusting* her to save the world. Sisu concentrates the magic into a glowing gem and blasts the Druun away, reviving the people of Kumandra but not its dragons. Riddled with fear, the people of Kumandra fight for possession of the gem. Naturally, their greed and violence separate them into tribes all named after the body part of a dragon in relation to their placement along a gigantic dragon-shaped river—Fang, Heart, Spine, Talon, and Tail.

Five hundred years later, the leader of heart, the tribe that possesses the gem, hosts a peace gathering. Raya, the Chief of Heart's daughter, befriends Namaari, the Chief of Fang's daughter. The girls quickly warm up to one another because of their shared fascination with dragons. Trusting Namaari, Raya decides to show her the top-secret location of the gem. I didn't see this coming, but the little girl Namaari is operating as a spy! Namaari turns on Raya, signaling her tribe to steal the gem once its location has been revealed. A fight of epic proportions ensues, and the gem is broken into five pieces, which releases the Druun.

Most of the inhabitants of Kumandra are now stone relics. Six years later, Raya finds Sisu chilling at the end of the dragon river, and the two dedicate their lives to eradicating the Druun by reuniting the five pieces of the gem possessed by each of the five tribes. In their pursuit of the gem pieces, they encounter quirky characters from across Kumandra. Together, they grieve the loss of their loved ones to the Druun, but their connection through the power of hope is much stronger. People from all tribes come together to help Raya and Sisu accomplish their heroic mission.

To make a long story short, the last piece of the gem is in Namaari's possession. Of course, it is! Disney loves the drama and the suspense. Raya cannot overcome her mistrust of Namaari after what happened in their childhood—do you blame her? But Namaari's whole heart is convicted when she sees Sisu's majesty for the first time. In a hold-your-breath moment, when all things could go right—all things go wrong! Of course, Namaari must accidentally kill Sisu—go figure!

In the final scene, the Druun swarm the village, turning light into darkness. The magical glistening of the gem pieces wards off the Druun, but the Druun quickly multiply until those who are in possession of a gem piece are encircled by the foreboding darkness. Because of some serious trust issues, the characters are reluctant to give up their piece of the gem so that it can be made whole once more. To our surprise, or at least mine, Raya is the first to muster the courage to entrust her piece of the gem to Namaari, of all people. And just like that, Raya turns to stone. Following Raya's lead, everyone else surrenders their fear to trust and love, as they too entrust Namaari with their piece of the gem.

Surrounded by stone figures, Namaari is in the exact same position as Sisu was hundreds of years prior. See how the universe teaches us if we choose to be in tune with it? Namaari reassembles the gem and everyone de-stones—sort of like defrosts, but with stone. The best part is that all the adorable dragons come back to life and frolic in the sky, creating beautiful color patterns. Kumandra lives happily ever after. I can say that with confidence because I do not foresee any pending sequels, per my last Google search.

Raya and her friends literally had to neurohack the instinctive fear program to survive. But they did more than survive; they prospered in love, peace, and harmony. Moreover, this movie further validates that we are all connected and part of the great mystery and magic of love and the only way to access it is through the *love program—and you have VIP pass!*

But wait, it doesn't stop there—it becomes more dire if we choose to operate in the *fear program.* This story reflects our fear of missing out. Yup, I just addressed FOMO! We fear we will miss out on the important stuff, just as the inhabitants of Kumandra feared they would miss out on the possession of valuable resources if they didn't fight for the gem. Aren't we doing the same thing with the finite resources that we are depleting across the globe? It's a fight for who can be the first to obtain the depleting oil or possess the greatest nuclear power. We fear that we will not be enough or possess enough, so we destroy one another. It must stop, and it starts with you neurohacking the fear program. We cannot create in the magnificent way we were designed to when we are operating in fear.

Neurohacking

Here are some ways to neurohack the fear program and download the love program. Start by turning off your autopilot and turning on your learning mode to lay down new and adaptive neural networks. Be sure to reinforce these new neural networks through practice so that they can become the new programs of your subconscious mind.

Patterns of the subconscious mind: Your dysfunctional behaviors always leave a trail of destruction behind them. Sometimes it comes as a feeling you are left with after a heated encounter, thoughts you have in the aftermath, and repetitive conflict in certain relationships. We are creatures of habit, and we repeat patterns. We are also very good at "monkey-see-monkey-do!" There is a possibility that your patterns of behavior are the patterns of your parents, or those who raised you. Do yourself a favor: Ask the people closest to you what you can do to improve your relationship with them. This will only work if you are receptive and genuinely grateful for their feedback. If you are defensive and dismissive toward them, it will backfire on you. Examine their feedback to determine if it lines up with your experiences. This, of course, demands that you become vulnerable. But remember, vulnerability is the key that unlocks the door to freedom and happiness. Once you've identified your behavioral patterns, you are aware and accountable—and you can never become "conveniently" unaware of them, again. Now that you've identified the behaviors that keep you stuck and miserable, ask yourself what the thoughts are behind those behaviors. Remember, thoughts are like seeds that sprout your emotions and behaviors that will eventually flower into your experiences. Dysfunctional behaviors are the reaping of dysfunctional thoughts. If your thoughts are incongruent with the power of your "I AM" and the love program, it's time to change your thinking.

Dedicated decision & fantastic feeling: Remember, your electromagnetic signature, comprised of your thinking and feeling, is your direct line to the universe. Your thoughts and emotions shine bright with energy and information that communicate to the universe everything you wish to attract. Identify a *dedicated decision* of what it is you wish to manifest, then decide fully that you will achieve it and remain dedicated to your dream. Be specific about what it is you wish to achieve. You may even write it down in detail. Then find a *fantastic feeling* that you want to experience upon your dream becoming reality. Emotions that emanate from love always have the highest vibrational frequency. Gratitude is a fantastic emotion to experience, as it confirms your dream coming true before it is experienced in your 3D reality. The more we are grateful for what we have, the more we attract new things to be grateful for. Now, it's all fine and dandy until we become impatient. A week may go by without a sign of your dream becoming reality. You may begin to lose heart, and instead of projecting gratitude from a place of abundance, you project frustration from a place of lack. Remember, you will not miss what is meant for you. Keeping this in mind will help you get through the waiting, while keeping your electromagnetic signature bright and shiny so that it can attract your dreams at the perfect time. Just because you may believe that you are ready to receive the dream doesn't mean that the dream is ready for you—it may still need time to develop. Even when there is no sign of its arrival, show faith in what you want to manifest by preparing for it before it arrives. If you wish to manifest success but you prepare for failure you will get what you prepared for.

Engage the senses. Evoking the senses is a great way to bring us out of autopilot and into the present moment. During my time spent in higher education, I took full advantage of a phenomenon known as *state-dependent learning*. While I studied, I'd chew on cinnamon gum, and then when it came time to take my exams, I'd also chew on cinnamon gum. The state that you learn the material in is the state that you should recall the material in, as it helps with memory retrieval. Sometimes I'd change it up. I'd study with the scent of a particular oil on my wrist—either lavender or eucalyptus—then I'd take the exam wearing the scent. I found that it also helped to calm my nerves and center my breathing. Get creative!

__Imagination:__ Never, ever forget that your brain does not know the difference between a real and an imagined experience, though your mind is fully aware of what's happening. In chapter 8, you learned about mirror therapy to cure phantom pain—which works in a similar manner. Last chapter, you dove deep into how to use your imagination to get you unstuck from painful memories. Moreover, we discovered that imagining doing exercise resulted in statistically significant muscle growth. How can you use your imagination as your secret weapon? There is no manifestation without imagination. You need to see your future self to become your future self. Don't limit your imagination; set it free to become limitless! As Albert Einstein said, "Imagination is more important than knowledge. Imagination is the language of the spirit. Pay attention to your imagination and you will discover all you need to be fulfilled."

__New experiences:__ Do not live the same predictable year 50 times and call it a life. Sometimes you must force yourself to break the energetic bond between yourself and your past routines. These routines become our autopilot. To have a new experience, you must use nearly double the amount of energy to break the bond of the old routine. Being born to create does not mean living life on a re-run of yesterday and the day before. New experiences promote neurogenesis—the growth of new neurons that can be programmed however you like. You learn more about your multi-faceted "I AM" through new experiences. You can't have growth without new experiences. It's time to plant some new flowers in your brain garden!

__Shorten negative emotional refractory periods:__ As a psychologist, I have sat across from countless couples who have spent days or even weeks not talking to each other because of an argument. Most of them couldn't even remember why they were arguing in the first place. Pride and ego can damage our most valuable relationships. I always tell my couples never discuss hot topics when you are angry and defensive. Remember, when we are angry, the blood from our frontal lobe rushes back into the primitive brain, and that's when we lose our cool. Choose to never argue when your "lid is flipped." Instead, allow the blood to return to your frontal lobe so that you can communicate with compassion. Moreover, when your frontal lobe is engaged, you are better capable of finding solutions to your problems. Negative emotions like sadness and anger are normal to experience. They are clues to help us understand the source of our problem. It is imperative to acknowledge your painful emotions. Allow yourself to feel them, but never stay stuck in them. Sometimes it may be of benefit to give ourselves a timeframe for how long we will stay in that emotion before releasing it or transforming it. Depending on the circumstances, I usually give myself 30 minutes to one hour to experience my unpleasant emotions. For some experiences, I can channel my inner Elsa and just "let it go;" other times, it requires a deeper level of processing—but no matter what, I am mindful of my emotional experience as I work to bring peace and harmony to the situation.

Forgiveness: Did you really think that I'd spend two whole chapters writing about trauma and not address the critical topic of forgiveness? Forgiveness falls into the category of shortening our negative emotional refractory periods. Let's cut to the chase; forgiveness is far more of a benefit to you than those who have hurt you. Unforgiveness is like quicksand: The more you struggle with it the more it sucks you under, until it suffocates you. When you choose forgiveness over revenge, you set yourself free from the toxic energy of pain and suffering. When you hold unforgiveness over the heads of your transgressors, what does it do to them? A whole lot of nothing. The only person aware of you doing that is you—and it's costing you a ton of energy to do so. Some have described unforgiveness as drinking poison and expecting someone else to die from it. When you forgive someone, you are by no means saying that what they did was right—it was wrong, period. Forgiveness does not mean re-establishing a relationship with your transgressor. It is your responsibility to set healthy boundaries to protect yourself and your peace of mind. Forgiveness means that you are choosing to no longer allow your transgressor to consume anymore of your energy. You choose to cut your energetic ties to them, and by doing so, you set yourself free!

Last, sometimes we must forgive ourselves. Embracing self-forgiveness finally sets us free to fully invest our energy in raising our vibration to better ourselves and make the world a better place. Bottom line: People who are hurting hurt other people. Let's stop the energetic hurt from spreading like a poison. You are capable of neurohacking the flow of energetic hurt when confronted by it.

Eliminate the ego: There are many definitions of ego. Let's look at it through the lens of superiority and excessive pride. The ego operates from the *fear program*, often separating itself from others to prove itself as being superior or distinguished. It is often attached to a narcissistic personality. Oddly, the ego is a defense mechanism formed in response to the belief *I'm not enough.* The ego works to overcompensate for a feeling of unworthiness. Most times, a haughty ego is a defense mechanism, rendering itself incapable of observing its behaviors as a way of coping with low self-worth. All of us possess an ego—big or small. Never allow your ego to prevent you from learning and growing. Do not let your ego get in the way of receiving constructive feedback on how you can become better. No matter how enlightened we believe we are, we can always improve up until we take our final breath. Never allow your ego to get in the way of having compassion for others. We are neurobiologically wired to love and to be loved. Never let anything get in the way of that—even your ego.

Just breathe: Breath work is one of the most powerful and effective neurohacking tools that we too often underestimate. When we are stressed, scared, nervous, anxious, or worried, we breathe fast and shallow. This quick breathing is triggered by our sympathetic nervous system, which activates our fight-flight-freeze response—a mental and physical state that increases our cortisol (stress hormone) levels and eventually deteriorates our health. In fact, you can take yourself from a calm state to a nervous one simply by breathing fast and shallow. Alternatively, breathing deep and slow triggers your vagus nerve, which is responsible for activating the parasympathetic nervous system that works to calm you. Here are some benefits of deep breathing: reduces stress hormones circulating in the body; improves sleep, immunity, posture, and blood flow; serves as a natural painkiller; and reduces inflammation. I recommend engaging in deep breathing multiple times a day to receive the benefits listed above, as such practice enhances its effectiveness during times of high stress. Coupling deep breathing with prayerful visualization can be even more powerful.

Box breathing is a useful deep breathing technique, and it looks like this: inhaling slowly by filling your lungs with air for a total of four seconds; holding your breath for four seconds; exhaling slowly by releasing the air in your lungs for four seconds; and finally holding your breath for four seconds prior to repeating the process and beginning again with inhalation. Deep breathing increases oxygen to the cerebral cortex and can make you feel dizzy if you are a beginner. Many smokers falsely give cigarettes all the credit for making them feel relaxed, yet nicotine is a stimulant that is meant to stimulate you—that's not relaxing! The truth is that smoking is a deep breathing process. You inhale slowly, filling your lungs with smoke and air, you hold it, and then slowly exhale releasing the smoke. Now let's try that again, but without the smoke!

Most people only think about the power of deep breathing to help calm and soothe their anxious and worried minds. We often leave out the benefit of breathing quickly to help energize us. To improve our focus and concentration we can practice the breath of fire—a yoga-informed technique—wherein you breathe quickly, like a panting dog. The inhale is passive, and the exhale is powerful. This can take us from a sleepy state to an awakened state faster than a cup of coffee! There are all sorts of breathing techniques to explore, from self-soothing to energizing, and even for pain management.

Playful. Just like you take your dog on a walk every day, let your inner child out to play! Your inner child possesses the most beautiful view of the world through a lens of awe and wonder. Do not let your ego imprison your inner child. If you want to frolic in the flowers, frolic in the flowers—just don't get arrested for trespassing. I begin each of my keynote speaking events with a playful activity for the audience to partake in. Secretly, I am psychoanalyzing their behaviors. I notice three types of behavior. The first behavior is totally uninhibited, fully embracing their inner child and encouraging everyone else to let their inner child out to play! I love it. The next type of behavior is going through the motions, wanting to be totally set free but self-conscious and concerned about others judging them. Then the last type of behavior is the one that judges and scoffs at the fun, declining to participate because they are above such ridiculous child's play. Which one are you? Who do you think has more fun? Isn't life about maximizing your opportunities to have more fun? What's holding you back? Moreover, embracing the spirit of the inner child is a sign of resilience and self-confidence!

__Movement:__ During my writing process for this book, I ran approximately four hundred miles! First thing in the morning, I run to clear my head and to come up with creative ideas, and then I run during my breaks to stay focused. Running is bilateral stimulation, which means using the right and left side of your body—alternating each side equally. This helps the brain to process and digest information. We do this in our sleep, as we consolidate everything that we've downloaded and experienced throughout the day. This stage of sleep is called rapid eye movement (REM), wherein our eyes move back and forth in our heads—right and left, and so on. Bilateral stimulation includes walking, swimming, jogging, cycling, and even tapping. It helps us to use our whole brain. When I move my right hand, the left hemisphere of my brain is triggered and vice versa. This is a contralateral indication that takes place in the brain's corpus callosum. Movement, especially rhythmic movement, is fantastic for soothing our autonomic nervous system. The first thing we ever heard as we were developing in our mother's womb was her heartbeat. Movement produces Brain Derived Neurotropic Factor (BDNF), which promotes neurogenesis (new neuron growth), strengthens connections between neurons, and nourishes the myelin sheath (connections between neurons). This is so important when we are working to lay down new neural networks grounded in the love program. It helps to strengthen them so that they fire and wire more effectively and efficiently. Remember, our new neural networks need all the power they can get when working to override the old and maladaptive neural networks that have kept us stuck.

Creating together

The love program never misses a beat. It never fails. It always shows up and shows out! All we must do is trust it. When we trust, we let go of our fear in exchange for faith. You are working diligently to rewire your brain to the love program by neurohacking the fear program that has been so deeply engrained into our mindset since childhood. When we believe that we are abundant, there is no room for lack. Countries go to war when they are power hungry. Remember, hunger comes from a place of lack, which operates in the fear program. No amount of natural resources or material wealth will ever satiate greed which comes from the fear of missing out (FOMO). Remember, abundance is a feeling that comes from within. It comes from being connected to the one true source—love. We are neurobiologically wired to love and to be loved. Love wires us for connection but fear wires us for protection. There is no trust in fear when we are constantly guarding ourselves— operating in survival mode. Making the world a better place starts with making yourself better. It starts with healing and rewiring your brain by connecting to the source of love and abundance. Our world needs to experience its very own version of Kumandra and, in doing so, raising the collective consciousness of our planet. We were also born to create *together*, and when we create *together*, the magic is multiplied!

Process Questions

> ➤ Who can give you valuable feedback on your behaviors in the context of your relationship with them?
> ➤ How can you be more playful?
> ➤ When can you schedule deep breathing during your days?
> ➤ How long are your negative emotional refractory periods?

> > o How can you shorten them?

> ➤ Create a vision board.
> ➤ Has your ego been getting in the way?

> > o How can you keep it in check?

> ➤ What new thing can you try? How frequently do you try new experiences?

Freedom Rhythm

> ➤ Please turn to page 180 to read about Freedom Rhythm and how to perform it.
> ➤ <u>**Transformation Zone 3:**</u>

> > o **<u>Visualization with bilateral stimulation:</u>** *I want you to visualize yourself in harmony with everything and everyone around you. If you need to transform negative energy— transform it!*
> > o <u>The mindset that informs your creative movement:</u>

> > > ▪ <u>Dedicated Decision:</u> "I AM harmonious."
> > > ▪ <u>Fantastic Feeling:</u> "Peace and relaxation."

> > o <u>Positive Affirmation:</u> "I AM harmonious! Yes, I AM!" x 3

162

Chapter 12

INFINITY AND BEYOND

"Laughter is timeless, imagination has no age, dreams are forever."

"We keep moving forward, opening new doors, and doing new things, because we're curious and curiosity keeps leading us down new paths."

WALT DISNEY

WELCOME BACK, HERO! You have undergone some incredible evolution throughout the course of the Hero's journey—from revelation and transformation to atonement and now the return. This chapter crams in the most fascinating topic of our time, in my humble opinion—the quantum realm! Moreover, I have consolidated all the laws of the universe into one place so that you never miss a beat. As Maui would say, "You're welcome!"

Tell me, why after the Big Bang, the most catastrophic explosion ever, has so much order come from so much chaos? Something was responsible for the herculean effort that harmoniously unified all the forces of nature to create a masterpiece. The answer is energy—the intelligence of the quantum or unified field to which all things are interconnected. In the quantum realm all things are possible and infinite, and the only way to get there is to completely surrender the fear program and allow love to be our guide. Of course, this reminds me of a Disney movie! I told you Disney has all the answers. Let's explore the movie, *Soul* that debuted in 2020.

In New York City, pianist Joe Gardner is a middle school music instructor who is passionate beyond measure about playing professional jazz. He has worked hard to finally obtain a stable career with benefits, but his job is emotionally draining because it is not his one true passion—jazz performance. Joe's mother discourages him from his passion because it pays poorly and has zero job security. But one fine day, the universe grants Joe the wild opportunity to audition for his dream gig to play alongside the famous musician Dorothea Williams. Impressed by his talent, Dorothea hires Joe for that night's show. Elated by the experience, Joe walks the streets of New York on Cloud Nine, oblivious to everything around him, and that's when he falls into an open manhole into the sewer drain.

Joe lands on the pathway toward the bright white light of the "Great Beyond." He shockingly discovers himself to be a disembodied soul. Eager for what his musical future has in store, Joe fervently resists death and attempts to escape but ends up in the "Great Before," the realm where new souls are prepared for life on Earth. Truly, Joe has entered the quantum realm. In fact, the new souls are guided by "counselors"— all named Jerry. My favorite quote in this movie comes from a Jerry who explains to Joe what he/she is: "I am the coming together of all quantized fields of the universe appearing in a form your feeble human brain can comprehend."

Desperate to get back to Earth, Joe offers to mentor a soul who is identified as 22. This soul has been mentored by all the most famous people in history and has remained in the Great Before for thousands of years in hopes of avoiding Earth. 22 must find her "spark" before she can inhabit an earthly body. Joe finds a way to cheat the system to return to Earth, but when he finally does, Joe falls into the body of a therapy cat, while 22 inhabits Joe's body.

Immediately, 22 falls in love with being a human, from savoring greasy pizza to watching a sycamore seed propel down from a tree in the gentle breeze. Her ability to connect with and enlighten other souls while in Joe's body brings 22 tremendous joy—so much so that she doesn't wish to leave Joe's body. In a turn of events, 22 is kicked out of Joe's body, and his soul is returned to experience an exceptionally successful concert with Dorothea Williams, who invites him to become a permanent member of her band.

Joe is pleased with the outcome but lacks the fulfillment he had hoped for. He returns home to his piano and pours over all the little "mundane" things that 22 collected and left in his pockets. 22 found these items to be magical. Feeling deep compassion for 22, Joe decides to allow her to swap positions with him. Joe begins to play piano so passionately that he enters a trance known as the "zone," which transforms into an alternate portal into the quantum realm. Joe searches for 22, who has experienced emotional suffering since being ejected from his body. Once 22 is found, Joe shows her the sycamore seed to remind her of the joy of life. The two come to recognize that a "spark" is one of many reasons for wanting to live. 22 excitedly agrees to return to Earth. As Joe prepares to enter the Great Beyond, a Jerry intercedes and offers him another chance at life for finally inspiring 22—the most challenged soul of all time—to live! 22 receives another body to inhabit, while Joe is granted the blessing to return to his body on Earth. This time, he is committed to living life to its fullest, savoring the smallest of moments—just as 22 had taught him!

I could spend the entire chapter dissecting the beautiful movie, *Soul* to show all the ways the laws of the universe were at play, from the law of harmony to the law of non-resistance. The biggest take-home is making the time to find your sparks—your reasons for living. You should collect sparks as eagerly as a child collects eggs on Easter. If your divine design for your divine destiny has not yet been revealed to you, the best thing you can do is collect sparks and indulge in them, as they operate as guides that will eventually lead you to your destination.

Naturally, this movie is bursting with existential passion, but I chose it because of all the time that is spent in the quantum realm, which is a state of consciousness that can be achieved by all of us. We observe this when Joe enters the "zone" while passionately enveloped in his piano playing. In this state, Joe slows downs his brain waves but remains consciously aware all at the same time. This is a magical place of existence that works to help us manifest our dreams, as well as heal our bodies. In this movie, we learn that the soul is meant to create all sorts of beautiful energetic connections that brighten our electromagnetic signature.

Quantum

Accessing the quantum realm is the ultimate neurohacking experience because it is the dimension of true creation—a never-ending unfolding of limitless potentials made solely of energy. The only way to enter this realm is through our conscious awareness while in a state of deep meditation. Wow, that sounds like an oxymoron, but you will come to understand it.

You and I live in a three-dimensional universe. This space is comprised of living organisms (us), places, objects, and time. When you break it down to the basics, we exist in a dimension of particles and matter, all of which we experience through our five senses—seeing, hearing, tasting, smelling, and touching.

According to the study of astrophysics, our universe is comprised of matter, and surrounding that matter is an infinite amount of space. Imagine your living room and notice the space between the furniture—do you see how there is more space than actual matter? I won't ever forget how I felt the night I stared out at the ocean, standing there alone with my thoughts, hypnotized by the sound of the waves. The black sky and the ocean blended seamlessly into an abyss that occasionally glistened in the moonlight. I felt like a tiny speck—so small in comparison to the vastness all around me. I allowed myself to almost evaporate into this beautiful and profound energy, as I felt connected to something far larger than myself. It was intimidating at first, because you must surrender your control to become connected. But once connected, trust was imminent, and with it, love and peace came flooding over me. This vastness of space is NOT nothing! It is EVERYTHING. It is an energetic field of information that never stops. It is the glue that connects all things. There is infinitely more of it than all the physical matter in all of existence.

Now back to the hard science: Newtonian physics is based on knowns and the predictable outcomes on the effects of matter as it relates to space and time. This includes measurements such as speed, distance, velocity, acceleration, force, density, mass, and length. Every material thing that we choose to observe is concrete and measurable. In our 3D world there is more space than time. But what about everything in between all of that? How do we measure a realm wherein there is more time than space?

If Newtonian laws are the outward expression of the laws of nature, we could surmise that the quantum laws are inversely related. Hence, the inward expression of the laws of nature is the unified field of information and energy that is the quantum realm. Instead of being captive to the space-time continuum, there is more time than space in the quantum realm. It is a dimension wherein time is eternal.

Buzz Lightyear knows exactly what I'm talking about! He experienced the quantum realm when he volunteered to be a test pilot for the hyperspace fuel crystal. After a four-minute test flight, Buzz discovers that four years have elapsed on the planet from which he originally departed—the result of time dilation, potentially governed by the quantum principles of superposition. Like I said, Disney apparently has all the answers to the universe.

Let's examine this all the way down to the level of an atom, the building block of life, even more basic than our genes. In case you were wondering, cells are the smallest forms of life, made up of atoms. An atom has a nucleus surrounded by a large field that contains one or more electrons. The field surrounding the atom is so vast when compared to the tiny electrons floating within it. If you were an electron, it'd be like you floating in the entire Pacific Ocean! It gets more interesting...

Researchers have discovered that the electron behaves in a totally unpredictable manner! Like a magician, the electron is present one moment, and vanishes the next. Now this is wild: Researchers finally determined that electrons exist simultaneously in an infinite number of possibilities and outcomes. The invisible field of energy and information collapses into a particle that we identify as an electron *only* when the person in search of it focuses their attention to find it. This is considered a quantum event—more specifically, collapsing the wave function. When the observer no longer focuses their attention, the electron vanishes back into energy. What if we can take this event that operates in a microcosm at the subatomic level and perform it by focusing our attention with an intention to create any infinite possibility within our macrocosm—otherwise known as our 3D reality? This would be the true source of manifestation.

Recall that your electromagnetic signature is comprised of your thoughts and emotions that create an electromagnetic field that surrounds your body and interacts with the electromagnetic field of the earth and all that comprises the quantum field. Are you starting to feel at least the slightest bit of mind blown?

The big question is how do we experience the quantum realm to create and manifest our creation? You must enter a deep state of meditation wherein your brain waves slow down dramatically. The slower our brainwaves, the less our frontal lobe is activated and the more suggestable we become. Recall that this is the part of your brain that is constantly thinking—sometimes critically, sometimes not. Slow brain waves allow us to enter the limbic brain, which is connected to our subconscious mind. This meditation requires us to take our attention off everything as we know it. We peel our attention away from our body and senses, away from our problems, away from our identity, away from our environment so that we may go beyond our "self." Again, visualize it as though you were dissolving into the vastness to become one with it. This is where our consciousness is pulled away from the material world and into the unified field. Truthfully, I am learning to master this experience myself, as quieting the body can be a challenge, but in doing so, your mind becomes master as you no longer operate on past programs, yet your mind is present without overanalyzing the experience. It is an art of balancing our mind, body, and spirit. Research demonstrates that meditation has tremendous benefit for our physical health; see the findings from *Brain, Behavior, and Immunity—Health* (August 7, 2023):

- Length of meditation practice may influence susceptibility to and management of COVID-19.
- Blood plasma from meditators can limit viral infection in cultured lung cells.
- Meditation elevates SERPINA5, a major player in coagulation and the immune response.

In this state of oneness with the quantum, our brain and our heart become more coherent, syncing together for the benefit of our physical health and, of course, enhancing our electromagnetic signature, so it becomes a vibrational match to everything our heart desires. Since we are all connected to the unified field of the quantum realm, we can shift the collective consciousness of the world for the better, if we all work together. Research at the Heart Math Institute has proven that where large numbers of people are intentionally focused on energized emotions derived from love, it affects the global information field (quantum realm), producing a more coherent environment that has the power to offset planetary discord. We exist in the universe as unidimensional beings, yet when we cross the threshold into the quantum realm, we are transformed by the multiverse into multidimensional beings. Bottom line, there is so much that we have yet to discover and fully comprehend about our incredible universe and the more we learn about it, the more we discover about ourselves, as we are a magnificent creation.

The Laws of the Universe

Love is the source of all abundance and blessing. It is the divine. There is no fear in love—nor is there anything negative or oppressive in its existence. Love is pure energetic light, and in it is everything that fulfills and nurtures our soul. Love is the essence of our spirit, which works to guide us for the purpose of bringing to fruition our divine design for our divine destiny, if we allow it. Let me reiterate that—if we allow it!

The blessings and abundance of love are pouring down upon us 24/7/365! You may be thinking, *If that's true, why am I not receiving this alleged blessing to the extent described?* I'm going to be a straight shooter in answering that question. You are failing to abide by any one of the laws of the universe. Let's use the law of forgiveness as an example. When you give your energy to unforgiveness, it's like holding up an umbrella to the abundant blessing that is pouring over you. You are causing blockage! The more you oppose the laws of the universe, the more umbrellas you hold up, which means the more you block your blessings. As soon as you forgive yourself and your transgressors, the unforgiveness umbrella is closed, which now gives you greater access to your blessings. You must dive deep into self-introspection to learn what umbrellas are blocking your blessings and why. If you ask, the divine spirit of love will guide you to the answers, but you must do the work.

In yoga, it is taught that we create the blockages of energy flow within the seven chakras of our body. Yoga teaches how to make breakthroughs physically and mentally. The same energetic blockages occur for the same reasons—not flowing with the laws of the universe. When we flow with the laws of the universe, our energy flows in all the right ways, which is beneficial for our health. However, when we force against the laws of the universe, our energy becomes blocked, creating densities within our bodies that are deleterious for our health. Recall for a moment the topic of epigenetics and how the energy of our thoughts and emotions can either up-regulate or down-regulate our genetic expression. There are laws to the game of life, and you absolutely need to know how to play the game to create the life of your dreams. For those inclined to religion—consider that the Creator of the universe is the One who created the laws, as they are also found in scripture.

- **Law of Love:** Allow love to rule and reign in your life. Love those who seem to stand in the way of your good—if you don't, they will continue to obstruct your destiny. Remember, love is an energy and vibration. All you must do is send love and light in their direction through your thoughts and emotions.
- **Law of Attraction (Vibration):** Everything in the universe is energy vibrating at a particular frequency. Our thoughts and emotions determine our energetic vibration. Whatever energy you put out into the universe is what will return to you—like a boomerang. The energy of your thoughts and emotions produces your electromagnetic signature, which is like a magnet. You can

only attract equal to or greater than the vibrational frequency you project.

- **Law of Karma:** Every action and every thought we behold will come back to us—good or bad. The law of karma reasons that our actions have commensurate consequences that will manifest in due time. The law of karma contains the principles of the law of attraction, with an emphasis on *consequences.*

- **Law of Forgiveness:** Thankfully, there is the law of forgiveness, by which we can cancel out the energy of our mistakes. As you guessed, this law is grounded in the love program. Asking for forgiveness is acknowledging that you did not abide by the rules of the love program and that your thoughts or actions were wrong. Forgiveness allows us to clean our karmic slate.

- **Law of Freedom:** Through truth we are set free of all karmic debts to act out the divine design for our lives. The truth shall set you free!

- **Law of Grace:** This is the best part: When you operate in the love program, you get access to several "Get Out of Jail Free" cards. This means that you don't get what you deserve—and this is a miraculous concept if you were a bad boy or bad girl! You get grace and favor over the law of karma. The law of grace is the unearned, undeserved, unmerited favor of the divine spirit of love.

- **Law of Harmony:** Harmony is only activated when one surrenders to the law of love. It is the phoenix rising from the ashes. It works to transform disorder into order. Even when bad things happen, it works to transform them into good.

- **Law of Gratitude:** Once we express gratitude for what we have and what we will manifest, our vibratory frequency is automatically and instantly switched to a positive vibration which attracts more things and situations for us to be grateful for.

- **Law of Non-resistance:** You have undoubtedly heard the words "what you resist persists." You've also read my phrase "flow—not force." When we resist something, we are creating an opposing force that we will eventually struggle against, and the more we struggle against it, the more power we give it.

- **Law of Prosperity:** If you wish to expect wealth, prepare to give generously. Order is the law of prosperity. If your finances and your home are in disarray, do not expect to attract prosperity. There is a supply for every demand when we trust in the divine spirit of love. Never ignore the urge or impulse to give; act upon it. When you do, the divine spirit of love uses you to bless others, as it will bless you.

- **Law of Substitution:** This occurs when we substitute our idea of "what should be," instead of embracing the way ordered by the divine spirit of love. An example of this is when Joe forces the motions of being a classroom music teacher over pursuing his dream of become a performing jazz pianist. When choosing the "safer route," such as the stable job with benefits, you let go of the possibility of manifesting your divine design for your divine destiny. When you trust in love to make the way, it will—but as soon as you lose trust, you obstruct the blessing.

- **Law of Faith:** Faith is trusting in the laws of the universe that are grounded in love and truth to do exactly what they are meant to do. Essentially, it is believing in the unseen and trusting in the unknown as though it were already seen and known that everything you desire has manifested in your three-dimensional reality. As soon as you begin to doubt, you weaken your electromagnetic signature, which is the energetic bond between you and the universe—the direct line to manifestation.

- **Law of Synchronicity:** When you are on the right track to fulfilling your divine design for your divine destiny, the universe will let you know by confirming it with signs that bring you joy. It could be hearing your favorite song on the radio at just the right time, seeing your favorite number appear more than once, or stumbling upon a quote that provides the perfect advice for that particular moment. The law of synchronicity is the universe winking at you and saying, "it's all working out in your favor!"

- **Law of Use:** The law of use tells us that we should use the things we buy and then discard them or donate them. Keep everything in your life flowing—even your finances. The congestion of things causes a congestion in our flow of energy.

- **Law of Intuition:** Intuition is the perfect guide, and it comes from your superconscious mind, the home of your "I AM." Often we call it a hunch. It's a strong feeling in the center of our chest that pulls us like a magnetic force to do something for our benefit. Intuition is a spiritual power and does not explain but points the way.

- **Law of Zero Losses:** Nothing can be lost in divine mind and abundance. What belongs to you by divine right is never lost—it will reappear at the right time and with faith. If you convince yourself that your loss is indeed a loss—so it will be. However, if you keep the faith and remember that what is yours by divine right can never be lost—it will find a way to return to you. Often, when it reappears, it returns multiplied for your benefit.

- **Law of Surprises:** When you have made your demand of what it is you desire to manifest, be ready for surprises. Everything may seem to be going wrong when it is really going right.

- **Law of Expectancy:** We can only receive what we see ourselves receiving. You cannot give or receive more than your subconscious mind believes is possible. This is the *law of expectancy and limitation.*

- **Law of Completion:** All ideas that are rooted in the energy of love are always brought to completion, if we do what needs to be done. Do not impede the law of completion by losing faith and fearing incompletion. Prior to the arrival of your manifestation, show faith by preparing for it and giving thanks for it—even when there is no sign of it!

Hit delete on the fear program. It is a mindset that will always keep you stuck, and it is indeed the biggest obstacle between you and your divine design for your divine destiny. Again, fear is important only when you are in a life-threatening situation. Trust that you will survive because your body knows exactly how to respond. Absolutely stop fearing things that do not pose a threat to your existence. Stop imagining worst case scenario: F (False) E(Evidence) A(Appearing) R(Real). Moreover, close all those umbrellas that you are holding up. Your blessings and abundance are waiting to saturate every space of your existence. Take off the blinders and work toward discovering your truth so that you can be set free.

Now is the time to live fully immersed in the love program. Stand firm in believing your great "I AM!" You are limitless: Believe it—behave it—become it! Trust in the divine spirit of love to guide you. If you need something, call upon it! You have not because you ask not. Lead with love in everything you do. Brighten your electromagnetic signature with the thoughts you think and the emotions you feel. Shine so brightly that you can be seen from outer space. The shift in the world's collective consciousness starts with you. You can influence everything you believe you can influence. It only takes one person to light up the world with love and creativity. If Walt Disney could do it—so can you! Imagine wildly and believe that it will manifest into your 3D reality. Color the world from the inside out and never forget that you are the magic. You are the hero! It's time now. You were born to create!

"All our dreams can come true, if we have the courage to pursue them."

WALT DISNEY

Process Questions

➢ Have you ever felt deeply connected with the universe? If so, when?

➢ When is a good time for you to practice meditating?

➢ What laws of the universe do you need the most improvements on? Why?

➢ What laws of the universe do you practice the most?

Freedom Rhythm

➢ Please turn to page 180 to read about Freedom Rhythm and how to perform it.

➢ **Transformation Zone 3:**

  o **Visualization with bilateral stimulation:** *I want you to energetically become one with the energy of love—the source that connects all things!*

  o The mindset that informs your creative movement:

  ▪ Dedicated Decision: "I AM love."
  ▪ Fantastic Feeling: "Love and gratitude."

  o Positive Affirmation: "I AM love! Yes, I AM!" x 3

THE LANGUAGE OF LIFE

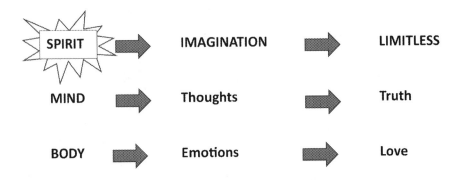

SPIRITUAL ORDER: The body must surrender to the mind, and the mind must surrender to the spirit. Grounded in truth and love, the **SPIRIT** shall lead the way, serving as the **COMPASS OF LIFE**.

The language of your **SPIRIT** is your **LIMITLESS IMAGINATION**.

The language of your **MIND (Soul)** are your **THOUGHTS** that seek **TRUTH**.

The language of your **BODY** are your **EMOTIONS** that emanate **LOVE**.

FREEDOM RHYTHM MANIFESTATION WORKSHEET

- My intention for manifestation is_____.

  o Is my intention formed in **love?**

    - How will my intention attract love into my life?
    - How will my intention attract love into the lives of others?
    - Am I allowing room for love to navigate the ultimate victory and fulfillment—even if it is somewhat different than what I envisioned?

  o Is my intention formed in **truth?**

    - How does my intention encourage me to embrace my true and authentic self?
    - Is my intention obtained in a truthful or honest manner?

  o What is my **"I AM?"**

    - Is my intention congruent with my "I AM?"
    - What "I AM" statements align with my intention?
    - What "I AM" statements do I need to build more confidence in?

  o How does my intention promote **peace and harmony** in my life and the lives of others?
  o What percent of your intention is **ego-centric?**

    - Are you comfortable with your answer? Why?

- ○ Am I forcing this intention or am I allowing it to **flow** as it is meant to be?
- ○ What **umbrellas** am I holding over myself that are **preventing** me from receiving the full downpour of my **blessings?** See page 169 for the complete rundown of the laws of the universe.

  - ▪ Law of Love, Law of Attraction, Law of Karma, Law of Forgiveness (self/others), Law of Freedom/Truth, Law of Grace, Law of Harmony, Law of Non-Resistance, Law of Prosperity, Law of Substitution, Law of Faith, Law of Use, Law of Intuition, Law of Zero Losses, Law of Surprises, Law of Expectancy, & Law of Completion
  - ▪ How will you **close** the umbrellas you identified?

- ○ Based on your answers, how do you need to **revamp** your intention for manifestation?

- My revised intention for manifestation has now become my **dedicated decision** which is_____.

  - ○ The **fantastic feeling** that I choose to increase my vibrational frequency is_____.
  - ○ Create a specific and **detailed visualization** in your mind of your dedicated decision.

    - ▪ **Butterfly tapping** is when you crisscross your arms over your chest so that the right hand touches the left shoulder, and the left hand touches the right shoulder. Alternate your tapping—right, left, right, etc.
    - ▪ With your eyes closed and while butterfly tapping, visualize in as much detail as possible the **completed manifestation** of your dedicated decision. Do not forget to amplify your fantastic feeling during this visualization process.

- If your visualization was a reel and it needed a **thumbnail**—a single static image to represent the victory of your dedicated decision—what would it be?
- Practice a short cut by envisioning your **thumbnail** and simultaneously amplifying your fantastic feeling.

o **Prepare** for your dedicated decision before it arrives—even when there is no sight of it on the horizon. If you ask for success but you prepare for failure—you will absolutely get what you prepared for. How can you prepare for the manifestation of your dedicated decision?

o **Do the work** that must be done. Remember, you **reap what you sow!**

o Multiple times per day, allow your **thumbnail** to energize you and excite you.

o Every day, work to fully identify with your **"I AM" affirmations.**

o Every day, work to **close your umbrellas.**

o Every day, take several minutes to **visualize** your dedicated decision and fantastic feeling.

o Every day say, *"Divine spirit of love lead me to my divine design for my divine destiny and remove all barriers for me to enter my promised land of abundance and fulfillment."*

o Remember, you have not because you ask not. *"Divine spirit of love I need _____. I have faith that you will provide it at the perfect time, and I give thanks for your supply for every one of my demands."*

FREEDOM RHYTHM
Emotion Focused Movement

At the end of all chapters, there will be a Freedom Rhythm exercise that you can partake in. Before doing so, read this information so you can learn how Freedom Rhythm works and how to properly perform it.

➤ ***Website:*** www.freedomrhythm.org
   Please visit our website to watch the informational video and to purchase silks for your Freedom Rhythm movement.

➤ Freedom Rhythm is an emotion-focused movement method informed by the study of neuroscience. It capitalizes on the power of the mind through visualization and the body through movement, as it works to free us from the toxic emotions that have stolen our peace and our ability to connect with one another. Freedom Rhythm uses a variety of silks (streamers, fans, flags, etc.) to project our emotions in a beautiful and vibrant way, as we learn how to create a narrative that sets us free. Together we are a work of art. Each silk is like a brushstroke contributing to the masterpiece.

➤ ***Why Freedom Rhythm?*** Did you know that your brain generates more electrical impulses in one day than all the cell phones in the world combined? What are you doing with all that energy? Are you using it to your benefit or weaponizing it against you? Emotion literally means *energy in motion*. The electromagnetic chemistry of our emotions, good or bad, impacts every single cell in our body. The negative energy of our emotions triggers a cascade of toxic stress hormones that down-regulate our genes. In contrast, positive emotional energy can be transformative for us and those around us, as it releases life-sustaining neurochemicals. Freedom Rhythm works to transform or expel our negative emotional energy, while harnessing and amplifying our positive emotions. It is a tool to improve our physical and psychological well-being. Dr. Bessel van der Kolk asserted that the body keeps score of painful life experiences. Now is that a score you want to keep? I don't think so! Let's zero the score by neurohacking our brain with Freedom Rhythm.

➤ ***How does Freedom Rhythm work?*** Suppressing our emotions results in psychological congestion, which is terrible for our physical health. When we become stuck on unresolved emotional pain, we live on autopilot for approximately 95% of our lives. To break free, the mind and the body must come together to expel the negative emotional energy that keeps us stuck. Apart from the body, the mind cannot fully achieve harmony on its own—and vice versa. The mind achieves freedom by altering its thoughts, while the body is set free through movement. We need both! We discover freedom of movement when we share our positive emotions and when we expel our negative emotions or simply transform them into productive energy.

Freedom Rhythm is the first and only emotion-focused movement protocol to engage the whole body, the senses, and the entire brain. It capitalizes on the power of the mind through visualization and the body through movement as it works to free us from toxic memories and emotions that have stolen our peace. Freedom Rhythm is informed by the study of neuroscience and uses visualization, bilateral stimulation, and movement to replace our old and unproductive neural networks with healthy and adaptive ones. Moreover, rhythm helps to soothe us. After all, we were developed to a rhythm—the beat of our mother's heart.

Freedom Rhythm uses a variety of silks to project our emotion in a beautiful and vibrant way, creating a story that sets us free. You are the choreographer, and your silk is the dancer. This sort of novel and playful movement pulls us out of autopilot and brings us back to the mindful moment—the only place wherein we can make positive change. You choose the physical intensity of your Freedom Rhythm: It can be a workout or a gentle meditative state. Drawing from evidence-based practices, Freedom Rhythm is a unique, creative, and imaginative approach to experience emotional release through authentic expression of movement. Be free. Be you!

The Five Elements of Freedom Rhythm

I. CONFRONTING THE HURT TO MOVE ON: The only way out is through. These words accurately depict the process of healing from painful life experiences. Hurtful events leave behind painful memories that are poisonous to our existence (psychological, spiritual, and physical) and impede our ability to heal. In fact, most people create poisonous narratives around their painful life experiences. Such narratives promote shame, guilt, regret, fear, and self-directed anger and hate—all of which result in self-destruction. Our memories become entangled in our toxic narratives, which evolve into our perception of truth—a poisonous lie that must be extracted, and the only way to extract it is to confront it. We must work to transform our toxic narratives into narratives that set us free.

II. RHYTHM: The mind and body are comforted by rhythm. As we formed in our mother's womb, we developed to the rhythm of her heartbeat. We are emotionally and physically regulated by rhythm. When we are anxious, we tend to tap our hands or feet, bounce our knees, or even rock back and forth to soothe ourselves. Rhythm has a calming effect on our minds, as it helps to regulate our autonomic nervous system (fight or flight response). Our goal in life is to fall into the right rhythms for our spiritual, psychological, and physical health.

III. BILATERAL STIMULATION: Have you ever noticed how your brain goes a million miles per hour when you're on a walk, jog, or run? Most of us come up with our best ideas during that time. This movement has an ingrained rhythm to it, in addition to a right and left movement (bilateral stimulation). Engaging in bilateral stimulation triggers both the right and left hemispheres of the brain, activating the brain's processing system. In the same way that the stomach digests food, the brain must digest thoughts, emotions, and experiences. Essentially, bilateral stimulation serves as a catalyst to the brain's digestive system, integrating thoughts and emotions stored in both of its hemispheres. In fact, the stage of sleep known as Rapid Eye Movement (REM) is a perfect example of this. During REM, your eyes move back and forth in your head as your brain digests and processes your experiences. This is effective in aiding long-term potentiation and memory consolidation. However, during REM (bilateral stimulation), we are asleep and therefore unconscious. Can you imagine how powerful bilateral stimulation is when we are consciously aware of what we're choosing to process/digest? Recall for a moment that our mind prefers to avoid hurtful experiences. Yet if we choose to confront those hurtful events for the purpose of changing the toxic narrative, a combination of bilateral stimulation and rhythm will help to reduce the psychological indigestion. It will also aid in consolidating the new and healthy narrative you create around your painful experience—a process that will help you find peace. Research informs us that bilateral stimulation helps us to re-integrate our painful/scary experiences, stored in the fear center of the brain (amygdala), into our regular, non-triggering, not scary, long-term memory (hippocampus).

IV. IMAGINATION/VISUALIZATION: Albert Einstein once said, "Imagination is everything! It is the preview of life's coming attractions." Everything we possess today has come from someone's imagination. The Bible says, *For as a man thinketh in his heart, so is he*

(Proverbs 23:7). If you imagine yourself as successful and blessed, so it will be. If you imagine yourself as the opposite of that, so it will be, too. In our minds, imagination can help us to rescript hurtful experiences and replace the past pain with hope and compassion, aiding in our psychological digestion and processing. Believe it or not, the brain has a difficult time detecting the difference between real and imagined experiences, both of which lay down neural networks that can promote adaptive changes in our thoughts and behaviors. Experiments conducted by neuroscientist Dr. Kelly Cole demonstrate that the mere visualization of exercising certain body parts can result in an increase in muscular strength in those areas of the body—and transforms the wiring of the brain's motor cortex just as actual physical exercise would.

V. <u>MOVEMENT:</u> Movement, especially rhythmic movement, is fantastic for soothing our autonomic nervous system. Movement produces Brain Derived Neurotropic Factor (BDNF), which promotes neurogenesis (new neuron growth), strengthens connections between neurons, and nourishes the myelin sheath (connections between neurons). This is so important when we are working to lay down new neural networks grounded in the love program. It helps to strengthen them so that they fire and wire more effectively and efficiently. Remember, our new neural networks need all the power they can get when working to override the old and maladaptive neural networks that have kept us stuck.

How do I practice Freedom Rhythm?

1.) Find a quiet place where you feel comfortable meditating and moving.
2.) Have your silk available. Freedom Rhythm silks may be purchased at www.freedomrhythm.org
3.) Be seated and begin focusing on your breathing.
4.) Bilateral stimulation positions to choose from:

a. Rest your right hand on your right leg and your left hand on your left leg and tap on your thigh—right, left, right, left, etc.

b. The butterfly hug is a position wherein you crisscross your arms over your chest so that the right hand touches the left shoulder, and the left hand touches the right shoulder. Alternate your tapping—right, left, right, etc.

c. Tap at your own unique rhythm and in a way that is comfortable for you.

5.) Read the visualization prompt and begin the visualization with your eyes closed or open, depending on how you feel most comfortable. Be sure to engage bilateral stimulation while in your visualization. These prompts are called *Transformation Zones.*

a. Stay in your visualization for about one minute and return to the present moment when you are ready.

6.) Each movement identifies a _dedicated decision_ and a _fantastic feeling_ for you to focus on. Take your silk and put your experience into movement with the music of your choice. It is recommended that your music selection not contain lyrics so that you can project your own emotional experience onto it. Allow yourself to spend as much time as you need in this movement.

7.) End your movement by speaking your positive affirmation three times, followed by waving your silk in the motion of an infinity sign. For example, you will say aloud, "I am lovable!" and then wave your silk in the infinity sign while saying, "Yes, I am!" as confirmation. Do this three times.

Each chapter will have four Transformation Zones for you to practice. Transformation Zones 1, 2, and 4 will always be the same—because they are so important. Each chapter will provide you with the third Transformation Zone to fill in. This zone will be relevant to the content of the chapter. Here are Transformation Zones 1, 2, and 4. Please reference this page, as only Transformation Zone 3 will be at the end of each chapter.

- ➢ **Transformation Zone 1:**

  - ○ **Visualization with bilateral stimulation**: *I want you to notice any negative emotional energy in your body that may be described as tension or stress. I want you to surround this area of your body with love and light.*
  - ○ The mindset that informs your creative movement:

    - ▪ Dedicated Decision: "I AM Free!"
    - ▪ Fantastic Feeling: "Freedom."

  - ○ Creative movement: Now, put your experience into movement with your silk. Silks can be purchased at www. freedomrhythm.org
  - ○ Positive affirmation: "I AM free! Yes, I AM!" x 3

- ➢ **Transformation Zone 2:**

  - ○ **Visualization with bilateral stimulation**: *I want you to notice all your blessings and anything you are grateful for. I want you to amplify them in your heart and mind.*
  - ○ The mindset that informs your creative movement:

    - ▪ Dedicated Decision: "I AM grateful!"
    - ▪ Fantastic Feeling: "Gratitude."

  - ○ Creative movement: Now, put your experience into movement with your silk. Silks can be purchased at www. freedomrhythm.org
  - ○ Positive Affirmation: "I AM grateful! Yes, I AM!" x3

- ➢ **Transformation Zone 3:**

  - ○ **Insert from respective chapter here***

- ➤ **Transformation Zone 4:**

  - ○ **Visualization with bilateral stimulation:** *I want you to visualize your victory. See yourself becoming the person you have always dreamed of becoming. Observe yourself accomplishing everything you have dreamed of accomplishing. Now, I dare you to dream bigger. Remove any limitations in your mind—because those are the only limitations.*

  - ○ The mindset that informs your creative movement:

    - ▪ Dedicated Decision: "I AM victorious."
    - ▪ Fantastic Feeling: "Gratitude for the victory."

  - ○ Creative movement: Now, put your experience into movement with your silk. This time, you are doing your victory dance!

  - ○ Positive Affirmation: "I AM victorious! Yes, I AM!" x 3

DISNEY MOVIE SYNOPSES:

References from *movies.disney.com*

Elemental (2023): This film takes place in Element City, where fire, water, land, and air residents live together in harmony. The story introduces Ember, a tenacious, intelligent, and fiery young woman, whose friendship with a fun and happy-go-lucky guy named Wade challenges her beliefs about the world they live in. Together, Ember and Wade—a mixing of opposing elements—create a never-before-seen chemistry!

Encanto (2021): An extraordinary family, the Madrigals, live in a magical house (Encanto) hidden in the mountains of Colombia. The magic of Encanto has blessed every child in the family with a unique and magical gifting from super strength to miraculous healing. Only one child has failed to receive a gifting, Mirabel. But when she discovers that the magic surrounding the Encanto is in grave danger, Mirabel determines that she is the key to either unlocking destruction or restoration.

Frozen (2013): Fearless optimist, Anna, sets off on a journey of epic proportions to find her sister, Elsa, whose icy powers have trapped the kingdom of Arendelle in eternal winter. A rugged mountain man named Kristoff and his goofy reindeer, Sven, assist Anna on her adventure. Together, they face treacherous weather and terrain, mystical trolls, and a hilarious snowman named Olaf.

Inside Out (2015): Growing up can be a rollercoaster of ups and downs, and it's no exception for Riley, who is uprooted from her Midwest life when her father starts a new job in San Francisco. Like all of us, Riley is guided by her emotions—Joy, Fear, Anger, Disgust, and Sadness.

The emotions live in Headquarters, the control center inside of Riley's mind, where they influence the actions of her everyday life. As Riley and her emotions struggle to adjust to a new life in San Francisco, all chaos breaks out in Headquarters. Joy, the optimistic leader of the emotions tries to keep things positive, but the emotions clash on how to best navigate Riley's new environment.

Lightyear (2022): "Lightyear" follows the legendary space ranger, Buzz, on an intergalactic adventure to escape from the evil Zurg and his robot army.

The Lion King (2019): In the African savanna a future king named Simba is born. He idolizes his father, King Mufasa, and takes to heart his own royal destiny. But not everyone in the kingdom celebrates the new cub's arrival. Scar, Mufasa's brother covets the thrown and creates his own plans to sabotage the pride of lions. The battle for Pride Rock is one of tragedy that results in Simba's exile. With help from newfound friends, Simba will have to learn how to grow up and plot to take back his rightful throne.

The Little Mermaid (2023): Ariel is a lovely, free-spirited, and adventurous mermaid with an intense fascination with the human world. As the youngest of King Triton's daughters and the most defiant, Arial falls in love with Prince Eric during one of her many forbidden adventures to the surface of the ocean. While mermaids are prohibited to interact with humans, Ariel must follow her heart. She makes a risky arrangement with the evil sea witch, Ursula, which gives her a chance to experience life on land but ultimately places her life—and her father's kingdom—in peril.

Moana (2016): Three thousand years ago, the greatest sailors in the world voyaged across the vast Pacific, discovering the many islands of Oceania. But then, for a millennium, their voyages stopped, and no one knows why… Moana is a courageous teenager who, with the help from demigod Maui sails out on a daring mission to prove herself a master wayfinder for the purpose of saving her people and their island from disease and eventually death.

Monsters, INC. (2001): Lovable Sulley and his wisecracking sidekick Mike Wazowski are the top scare team at Monsters, Inc., the scream-processing factory in Monstropolis. When a little girl named Boo wanders into their world, it's the monsters who are scared senseless, and it's up to Sulley and Mike to keep her out of sight and get her back home before it's too late!

Ratatouille (2007): In one of Paris's most exquisite restaurants, Remy, a determined young rat, dreams of becoming a renowned French chef. Torn between his family's wishes and his true calling, Remy and his pal Linguini set in motion a hilarious chain of events that turns the City of Lights upside down.

Raya and the Last Dragon (2021): In the fantasy world of Kumandra, humans and dragons once lived together in peace and harmony. But when an evil force threatened the land, the dragons sacrificed themselves to save humanity. Without the dragons, the people divided themselves—warring over the last remaining remanent of the dragons' existence. Now, 500 years later, that same evil has returned and it's up to one lone warrior, Raya, to find the long-lost, legendary dragon to restore the fractured land and its divided people.

Soul (2020): Joe Gardner, a middle-school band teacher gets the chance of a lifetime to play alongside the most famous jazz musician of his time. Distracted by the good news, he carelessly falls into a pothole and finds himself in the "Great Before" where new souls get their personalities, quirks, and interests prior to transcending to Earth. Determined to return to his life, Joe teams up with a lost soul, 22, who is reluctant to have a human experience. As Joe desperately tries to show 22 the wonders of life, he discerns the answers to some of life's most profound existential questions that will determine whether he gets a second chance at life.

Wall-E (2008): After hundreds of lonely years of doing what he was designed to do, the curious and lovable Wall-E the robot discovers a new purpose in life when he meets a sleekly designed, hi-tech, search robot named EVE.

Wreck-It Ralph (2012): Burned out on playing the role of a bad guy in his video game, Ralph takes matters into his own massive hands and sets off on a journey across the arcade through multiple generations of video games to prove that he is worthy to be a hero and to be treated like one.

Ralph Breaks the Internet: Wreck-It Ralph 2 (2018): Ralph and his bestie, Vanellope, risk it all by traveling through the internet in search of a part to save her game, Sugar Rush. Overwhelmed by this new world and completely in over their heads, they must rely on the citizens of the internet. Yesss, the head algorithm and heart of the trendy site BuzzzTube, and Shank, a bad-to-the-bone driver from the hard-core online auto-racing game Slaughter Race—team up to help Ralph and Vanellope. This exhilarating new world with its exciting new friends calls out to Vanellope's soul. Does she answer their calling or return to what she knows?

Zootopia (2016): In the modern mammal metropolis of Zootopia, Officer Judy Hopps, the first bunny on the Zootopia's police force, is determined to prove herself worthy by jumping at the chance to crack her first case—an alarming unsolved mystery that is turning once gentle mammals into savages. Judy must partner with a scam-artist fox, Nick Wilde, if she wants to have a shot at cracking the case.

Printed in the United States
by Baker & Taylor Publisher Services